IN THE

FOOTSTEPS

OF FAITH

IN THE
FOOTSTEPS
OF FAITH

---

*Lessons from the Lives of
Great Men and Women of the Bible*

JOHN F. MacARTHUR

CROSSWAY BOOKS • WHEATON, ILLINOIS
A DIVISION OF GOOD NEWS PUBLISHERS

In the Footsteps of Faith

Copyright © 1998 by John F. MacArthur

Published by Crossway Books
      A division of Good News Publishers
      1300 Crescent Street
      Wheaton, Illinois 60187

Unless otherwise indicated, Bible quotations are taken from the New American Standard Bible, copyright © 1960, 1962, 1963, 1968, 1971, 1972, 1973, 1977 by the Lockman Foundation and used by permission.

Cover design: D² DesignWorks

First printing, 1998

Printed in the United States of America

ISBN 1-58134-019-2

Library of Congress Cataloging-in-Publication Data
MacArthur, John, 1939-
    In the footsteps of faith : lessons from the lives of great men and
women of the Bible / John F. MacArthur
        p.   cm.
    Includes indexes.
    ISBN 1-58134-019-2 (tpb : alk. paper)
    1. Christian life--Biblical teaching.   2. Bible--Biography.
I. Title.
    BS680.C47M33   1998
    220.9'2—dc21   98-34849
                                          CIP

11	10	09	08	07	06	05	04	03	02	01	00	99	98
15	14	13	12	11	10	9	8	7	6	5	4	3	2	1

CONTENTS

INTRODUCTION

Thomas Brooks said, "Example is the most powerful rhetoric." He was right. The single greatest tool of spiritual leadership is the power of an exemplary life. Along with the principles for living that the Bible gives us, we need models to follow because we tend to be creatures led more by pattern than precept. We are better at following a pattern or a model than we are at fleshing out a precept or principle.

What makes examples so powerful? Why is it "the most powerful rhetoric"? An example shows us what principles can't. Principles and precepts instruct us about our duty. But an example assures us the duty is possible because someone else is also performing it. If there wasn't anyone I could look to as a model of spiritual virtue, I could easily think such virtue is impossible. Wouldn't you? When you read the Bible and endeavor to obey its precepts, you come face to face with your own weaknesses, failures, and sin. That's when it's easy to become overwhelmed and conclude that being obedient to God's Word seems beyond you.

But when you can look at someone who models spiritual virtue, there is the reality that living a faithful life is attainable. Paul understood the importance of example. In Philippians 4:9 he says, "The things you have learned and received and heard and seen in me, practice these things." He said to Timothy, "Let no one look down on your youthfulness, but rather in speech, conduct, love, faith and purity, show yourself an example of those who believe" (1 Tim. 4:12). Peter followed suit, admonishing the church elders not to lord their authority over those in their charge, but to be godly examples (1 Pet. 5:3). As believers we need to follow in the footsteps of those who put flesh on principles and life into precepts—people we can pattern our lives after.

This book describes the lives of some of my favorite biblical leaders and servants of God who by their life pattern or in a significant event set an example of faithfulness to God through their obedience.

The writer of Hebrews said, "Now faith is the assurance of things hoped for, the conviction of things not seen. For by it the men of old gained approval" (11:1-2). People often confuse faith with a wistful longing that something, however unlikely, will come to pass in the future. But "assurance" points to facts or reality, as opposed to mere wishing. Faith based on God's Word focuses on absolute certainty.

The Old Testament saints had the promise of a coming Messiah who would take away sin. They believed God, even though their understanding of the Messiah was incomplete and somewhat vague. They knew their hopes would be fulfilled, and that assurance dominated their lives. These "men of old gained approval" from God because of their faith, and because of nothing else. God has always approved and recognized the person of faith. God makes His approval known to those who trust Him. How God shows His approval through blessing varies, but every saint has had God's witness that his faith is pleasing to his Lord.

It's the same for New Testament believers. Peter said, "Though you have not seen [Christ], you love Him, and though you do not see Him now, but believe in Him, you greatly rejoice with joy inexpressible and full of glory, obtaining as the outcome of your faith the salvation of your souls" (1 Pet. 1:8-9).

True faith trusts fully in its object. For the Christian, that means resting in God and His promises. And that's the primary characteristic of each faithful individual in this book. They all believed God and responded accordingly.

To give us a fair representation of the people of faith, I have chosen nine men and four women from the Old and New Testaments who obeyed God and thus proved their faithfulness in both great and small ways. We'll begin by looking at Noah who proved his faithfulness by obeying God's command to build something that had never been built before. We'll see that Abraham set the pattern of faithful living for an entire nation. And we'll see how Moses obeyed God in several important decisions.

Our first woman is Rahab, and we'll see how her protection of two of the Lord's spies earned her a place among God's faithful. Next we'll look to Hannah and see the magnificent example of a godly mother. We'll conclude our look at Old Testament saints by learning from the negative example of Jonah. He shows us how God can turn a stubborn, disobedient servant into a useful and faithful missionary.

To begin our New Testament examples, we'll look first to Mary, the mother of our Lord. She is an ideal example of how one should worship God. Then we'll look at our Lord's cousin—John the Baptist—and will see why Jesus called him the greatest man who had ever lived.

One of the more interesting examples of faith is someone we often associate with failures—the apostle Peter. But it is those failures that give us hope because Jesus used them to turn him into a faithful leader of His people.

Perhaps there is no greater example in the Bible than the apostle Paul. Jesus transformed him from a hater of the church into the greatest and most faithful leader it has known. One of Paul's converts was a woman named Lydia, whose brief appearance in Scripture encourages us that we all have received faith as a gift of God. No treatment of New Testament examples would be complete without Timothy, because he himself followed the example Paul set for him. He is thus a second-generation faithful servant. Another man who served faithfully with Paul and Timothy is a rather obscure individual named Epaphroditus. Yet his model of sacrificial service stands as a beacon for all would follow his path of humble faithfulness.

Finally, no book on spiritual models would be complete without some discussion of our Lord Jesus Christ Himself. He is our ultimate and perfect example of faith and humble obedience.

My prayer is that by the end of this study you will see how these great saints are patterns for your life, so that someone might be able to follow in your footsteps of faith.

1

NOAH:

A FAITH

THAT OBEYS

Throughout the centuries Satan has continually tried to confuse and mislead men and women, even believers, about the relationship of faith and works. He will attempt to convince people that they can be saved by doing good works. If that ploy is effective, those individuals will not be genuinely saved. And Satan will seek to persuade Christians to accept one of two extremes—good works are necessary to maintain salvation (legalism), or, because salvation is through faith, good works are unnecessary (license). Throughout Scripture, however, the Holy Spirit makes it clear that people are saved only by grace through faith; and when they are saved, good works will always verify their profession of faith. The apostle James illustrates it this way:

> *What use is it, my brethren, if a man says he has faith, but he has no works? Can that faith save him? If a brother or sister is without clothing and in need of daily food, and one of you says to them, "Go in peace, be warmed and be filled," and yet you do not give them what is necessary for their body, what use is that? Even so faith, if it has no works, is dead, being by itself.*
>
> *—Jas. 2:14-17*

If our faith in God is truly alive, we will show it in the way we live, in what we say, and in how we serve Him (cf. Jas. 2:26). The apostle Paul wrote that believers are "created in Christ Jesus for good works, which God prepared beforehand, that we should walk in them" (Eph. 2:10). All the saints mentioned in Hebrews 11, the Heroes of Faith chapter, proved the genuineness of their faith by standing for the truth and performing many good works. The patriarch Noah was no exception.

As Hebrews 11:7 states, Noah's life was perhaps more an illustration of obedient faith than was any one else's in history: "By faith Noah, being warned by God about things not yet seen, in reverence prepared an ark for the salvation of his household, by which he condemned the world, and became an heir of the righteousness which is according to faith." That verse suggests four things about Noah's life and faith: (1) he responded obediently to what God said; (2) the ark had great spiritual and practical significance; (3) his very life rebuked the world of wicked people who surrounded him; and (4) God gave him a legacy of righteousness.

NOAH'S RESPONSE TO GOD'S COMMAND

Noah was born and reared during a crucial transition period in the early history of the world. Genesis 5:28-32 indicates that he was the last pre-Flood descendant in the godly line of Adam through Seth (see also 5:1-27):

> *And Lamech lived one hundred and eighty-two years, and became the father of a son. Now he called his name Noah, saying, "This one shall give us rest from our work and from the toil of our hands arising from the ground which the LORD has cursed." Then Lamech lived five hundred and ninety-five years after he became the father of Noah, and he had other sons and daughters. So all the days of Lamech were seven hundred and seventy-seven years, and he died. And Noah was five hundred years old, and Noah became the father of Shem, Ham, and Japheth.*

During the early centuries of Noah's life, mankind's complete depravity and rebellion against God became so intense that "the

LORD was sorry that He had made man on the earth, and He was grieved in His heart. And the LORD said, 'I will blot out man whom I have created from the face of the land, from man to animals to creeping things and to birds of the sky; for I am sorry that I have made them'" (Gen. 6:6-7).

However there was great hope for Noah, as the text goes on to say: "But Noah found favor in the eyes of the Lord. . . . Noah was a righteous man, blameless in his time; Noah walked with God" (vv. 8-9). Expository commentator James Montgomery Boice describes the importance of Noah's advantageous situation in this way:

> Noah grew up in an environment of faith and by the grace of God became what he is said to have become. We are told, "Noah was a righteous man, blameless among the people of his time, and he walked with God" (Gen. 6:9). It was because of this that he was able to stand for God and with God against the ungodliness of the pre-Flood generation.
>
> How did Noah get to be blameless before God? To answer this question we must go back to the preceding verse, verse 8, where we are told, "But Noah found favor (or grace) in the eyes of the Lord." Some people read these verses as if Noah found favor with God because he was righteous and lived a blameless life. But that is not the case and, in fact, to read it that way is to get it backward. Verse 9 does not come before verse 8, nor is there even a connecting or causal participle between them, as if to say, "Noah found grace *because* he was righteous." Actually, Noah's righteousness was the product of his having found favor and is therefore the proof of that favor, not its ground.
>
> This is a great biblical principle, namely, that the grace of God always comes before anything. We imagine in our unsanctified state that God loves us for what we are intrinsically or for what we have done or can become. But God does not love us because of that, nor is He gracious to us because of that. On the contrary, He loves us solely because He loves us. He is gracious to us only because He is.

(*Genesis: An Expositional Commentary* [Grand Rapids, Mich.:
Zondervan, 1982], 256; emphasis in original)

Noah's solid standing before God enabled him to respond obediently to His command about building an ark: "Then God said to
Noah, 'The end of all flesh has come before Me; for the earth is filled
with violence because of them; and behold, I am about to destroy
them with the earth. Make for yourself an ark of gopher wood; you
shall make the ark with rooms, and shall cover it inside and out with
pitch'" (Gen. 6:13-14). When Noah received the initial instruction,
he immediately began constructing the ark, even though he likely
lived in Mesopotamia (in the so-called cradle of civilization, on dry
land between the Tigris and Euphrates Rivers), and thus God's words
undoubtedly sounded totally strange and absurd.

In addition, Noah would not have seen even a small flood prior
to God's command, because it probably did not rain before the
Flood, and floods occur because of rain. Thus as Hebrews 11:7 says,
Noah's response to God's words was entirely by faith, which is "the
assurance of things hoped for, the conviction of things not seen" (v.
1). God's command was enough for him to proceed with the
shipbuilding.

To most of us, God's command would have been embarrassing,
demanding, and overwhelming—to the point that we probably
would have done anything or offered any excuse to get out of following it. But Noah, who didn't possess all the written revelation we
have, did not question God, complain, or procrastinate. He simply
obeyed God and spent more than a century carrying out His directive. Noah is a supreme example of faithful perseverance in finishing
an incredibly enormous and strange assignment from the Lord.

To appreciate Noah's faith, you need to understand that he certainly had no idea what he was building—he wouldn't have known
what a large oceangoing ship looked like since no one had ever built
one before (and no one had ever seen an ocean before). And Noah
may not have had his sons' help, because Genesis 5:32 says Noah was
at least 500 years old when they were born. Therefore, Noah's chop-

ping down the first gopher wood tree for lumber was one of the greatest practical acts of faith in world history.

Hebrews 11:7 further says that Noah "in reverence prepared an ark." The Greek word for "reverence" can be translated "pious care or concern," which means that Noah acted with a sense of genuine spiritual devotion. He responded to God's message with great respect and awe. As we have noted, Noah was already a man of obedient faith (Gen. 6:9) when God directed him to build the ark. He had apparently been faithful over smaller things, and God gave him a much greater task to perform.

THE SIGNIFICANCE OF THE ARK

The precise physical dimensions of Noah's ark are uncertain. Using the most conservative figure, the cubit of Noah's day would have equaled 17.5 inches (the length established by measuring the distance from the elbow to the fingertips). That translates into an ark that was 438 feet long, 73 feet wide, and 44 feet high. It was almost one and a half times the length of an American football field and taller than a four-story building. The combined area of its three decks was nearly 96,000 square feet, and the total volume within those decks was approximately 1.3 million cubic feet. Such a massive vessel was not designed for style or maneuverability but for stability. Studies by modern naval engineers confirm that the ark's shape and dimensions form the most stable ship design possible.

Though the completed ark was actually a gigantic, seaworthy vessel, it also provides a spiritual analogy of God's redemptive dealings with all mankind. Robert S. Candlish presents this graphic and urgent picture:

> Look within the ark. There are prisoners there; and to the eye of sense, they are apparently shut up to die. But they are prisoners of hope; —they have fled to a stronghold; —they have that all around them through which no floods of wrath can penetrate;-their refuge is "pitched within and without

with pitch" (chap. vi. 14). It is well protected against the worst weather. And what an emblem is the pitch;-the very word meaning propitiation or the covering of sins by sacrifice;-of their complete security from every kind of terror, whether temporal or eternal, —from all risk of perishing either here or hereafter! They have pitch on all sides of their new dwelling; pitch within and without, —pitch, making it effectually a covert from the storm and a hiding-place from the tempest—even such as A MAN is to the sinner, —the man Christ Jesus (Is. xxxii. 2).

Look again without the ark. There are prisoners there, too, "spirits in prison;" condemned criminals, confined in the lowest vaults of that frail fortress on which the waves of wrath are about to burst. Do you see them, these prisoners, all alive and joyous, and affecting to pity the small company buried within the ark? Do you see them making merry, —or trying, by desperate gambling, to make gain?

Look once more and listen. There is a lightning flash, a rushing mighty noise. The flood comes. —In which of the two prisons would you have your spirit to be?

Thus, by the ark which he prepared, Noah "condemned the world." The warning which might have saved them, turned to their greater condemnation. But "he delivered his own soul" (Ezek. xxxiii. 9); and he prepared the ark to "the saving also of his house" (Heb. xi. 7). (*Studies in Genesis* [1868; Grand Rapids, Mich.: Kregel, 1979 reprint], 134)

From the outset, Noah's immense assignment to build the ark was inextricably linked with the covenant God would make with him (Gen. 6:18). That covenant would also be with "every living creature of all flesh that is on the earth" (9:16) that survived the Flood, including all mankind (the descendants of Noah and his sons). But the covenant was primarily with Noah, who had "found favor in the eyes of the LORD" (6:8). Candlish expands on the profound and far-reaching significance of God's covenant with Noah:

It might, indeed, seem [concerning the Flood] as if the Lord had forgotten to be gracious—as if in this unbounded and intolerable provocation, his mercy were clean gone for ever (Ps. lxxvii. 8, 9).

It is not so, however. God remembers his covenant: "But with thee will I establish my covenant; and thou shalt come into the ark, thou, and thy sons, and thy wife, and thy sons' wives with thee" (ver. 18). He is faithful and true; and though terrible in his righteous vengeance, he keeps covenant and mercy. And he has always some with whom he may establish his covenant; if not seven thousand who have not bowed the knee to Baal, at least one who finds favour in his sight. His purpose of love according to the election of grace stands sure, and all the unbelief of a world of apostates cannot make it void. The gracious covenant, into which at first, when all seemed lost, he admitted Adam as a partner, he will now again, in this desperate crisis, establish with Noah. And with excellent reason. For it is neither with Adam, nor with Noah, that the covenant is made, else with Adam at the fall, and with Noah at the flood, it must have been for ever ended. What righteousness or what power had either Adam or Noah in himself to save him from the general wreck and crash of a ruined world, and sustain him erect and fearless before the Righteous One? But the covenant is with his own beloved Son; and with Adam and Noah only in him. Hence it stands sure, being eternal and unchangeable. While the earth is moved, and the mountains shake with the swelling of the seas, the faith which God works by his Spirit in his chosen, enables Noah calmly to lay hold of the promise, that the Seed of the woman shall assuredly, in spite of all, bruise the head of the serpent. In Christ the Son—whose day, even amid the waste of waters, he sees, however dimly, afar off—he may appropriate the Father's covenanted love as his portion; and so doing he may be glad. (*Studies in Genesis*, 129-30)

The connection between the story of Noah and the Gospel is inescapable. As we stated earlier in this chapter, Noah was declared righteous, being justified by God's pure grace, applied through faith.

The apostle Paul refers to justification in the Old Testament when he quotes Genesis 15:6, "For what does the Scripture say? 'And Abraham believed God, and it was reckoned to him as righteousness'" (Rom. 4:3). The term "reckoned," also translated "imputed, credited, or accounted," had both a financial and legal meaning in the Greek language. It was a one-sided transaction in which something belonging to someone was credited to another's account. Simply because Noah and Abraham trusted in God, He took His own righteousness and credited it to them as if it were actually theirs (see Rom. 4:1-8).

NOAH'S LIFE REBUKES THE WORLD

Even before God called Noah, ancient society had become morally and spiritually bankrupt. Evil was more rampant than at any time in history. "The LORD saw that the wickedness of man was great on the earth, and that every intent of the thoughts of his heart was only evil continually" (Gen. 6:5). A second aspect of Noah's God-given assignment was to proclaim God's message of judgment, which would soon be unleashed on the people of that time because of their sin and unbelief. That's why the apostle Peter identified Noah as "a preacher of righteousness" (2 Pet. 2:5). As he built the ark, he was to warn the people of the impending wrath of God.

Mankind during Noah's time had become demon-possessed. I believe "the sons of God" in Genesis 6:2 were fallen angels, demons who indwelt men (cf. 1 Pet. 3:19-20). Their flagrantly sinful sexual intercourse with mortal women ("the daughters of men") demonstrates mankind's evil nature and how fallen humanity fell even further into sinful attitudes and practices. Such activity exhausted God's perfectly holy patience, so He prepared the severest of judgments—the destruction of the whole world of unrepentant sinners.

However, God never enjoys meting out judgment, no matter how deserving the recipients (Gen. 6:6; cf. 2 Pet. 3:9). He delayed the coming of the Flood for 120 years (Gen. 6:3) so Noah could warn the people and urge them to repent. The apostle Peter summarized the situation this way: "The patience of God kept waiting in the days of Noah, during the construction of the ark" (1 Pet. 3:20). As the Lord was preparing judgment (the Flood), He was also using Noah to prepare a way of escape and to exhort his neighbors to repent.

Noah's pre-Flood ministry was the culmination of a sequence of events in which the Holy Spirit did "strive with man" (Gen. 6:3). That sequence began with Abel's pleasing sacrifice, which testified to a proper worship of God (Gen. 4:4). Then Enoch's lifestyle exemplified true fellowship with the Lord (Gen. 5:24). In between was Cain's man-centered worship, his sinful resentment that led to murder, and God's punishment of him (Gen. 4:5-15). That should have been a constant reminder to subsequent generations of how God views sin.

In addition to those specific examples, God's natural revelation always testifies to His power and rule over mankind: "Since the creation of the world His invisible attributes, His eternal power and divine nature, have been clearly seen, being understood through what has been made, so that they are without excuse" (Rom. 1:20). By the time of Noah's ministry, people had already received abundant warning and sufficient opportunity to turn from their sins. Therefore, it's truly astounding that no one who heard Noah's message over 120 years repented and joined him and his immediate family in the safe confines of the ark.

In the midst of such challenging and discouraging circumstances year after year, Noah undoubtedly was tempted to put off or give up his God-ordained responsibilities. But he made no excuses to God about his lack of preaching qualifications or his lack of shipbuilding experience. He simply preached and built, as commanded, year after year, in the face of relentless ridicule, wicked rebellion, and callous indifference from the people. In spite of many unanswered questions and long years with no evidence of progress, Noah faithfully and continually obeyed God.

NOAH'S LEGACY

Perhaps the saddest lesson from pre-Flood days is how little things have changed in the world. God's message was rejected then; it is rejected today. Violence, immorality, dishonesty, rage, murder, profanity, blasphemy, and a general man-centered outlook prevailed then; the same things are widespread today. A small remnant found grace and mercy then; a relatively small number of people are believers today. People in the world have not changed their basic attitude toward God, and will not until Christ returns:

> *"For the coming of the Son of Man will be just like the days of Noah. For as in those days which were before the flood they were eating and drinking, they were marrying and giving in marriage, until the day that Noah entered the ark, and they did not understand until the flood came and took them all away, so shall the coming of the Son of Man be."*
>
> *—Matt. 24:37-39*

Noah's righteous life and obedient, faith-filled testimony shines in stark contrast to a wicked, cruel, and depressing world. His holiness serves to condemn those who rebel against God. The man of faith rebukes the world by his consistent life, even if he never utters a word of reproof.

Noah has left us a worthwhile and instructive legacy. He was the first person in Scripture to be called "righteous" (Gen. 6:9), and that righteousness proved that his faith in God was genuine. James Boice gives us this fitting summary of the impact of Noah's life:

> This solitary righteous man of the pre-Flood generation, Noah, is remembered throughout the world when virtually all his unrighteous contemporaries are forgotten. A "dog now," but vindicated later! Forgotten now, but remembered later! That is what Noah was. It is what every true believer should be willing to be.

There is this point too. Even though others should forget and never remember, we can know that God remembers and that He has caused "a scroll of remembrance," containing the names of those who fear and honor the Lord, to be recorded (Mal. 3:16). Was Noah forgotten by God? Not at all! (*Genesis: An Expositional Commentary*, 259)

2

ABRAHAM:

A PATTERN

OF FAITH

People can live life in one of two contrasting fashions. The approach that comes naturally to everyone is to live empirically—basing all their thoughts and actions on what they can see and experience. The other fashion, which does not come naturally to anyone, is to live by faith, to base life primarily and ultimately on what we cannot see or feel. The Christian, of course, is called to live by faith. He has never seen God the Father, the Lord Jesus Christ, or the Holy Spirit. He can't see heaven or hell. Nor has he talked to any of the Spirit-led authors of Scripture or read their original manuscripts. Believers cannot see the spiritual graces and virtues God gives, although they can see the results in themselves and in other believers.

Even though none of the preceding important principles and aspects of Christianity can be seen, as believers we are convinced by faith of their truthfulness, and we live accordingly ("by faith, not by sight," 2 Cor. 5:7). We base our present lives and future destinies on invisible realities. It has always been that way for the true followers of God.

The New Testament clearly states that Abraham was the first true man of faith. He is the spiritual father of all who believe (Gal. 3:7, 29). Pre-Flood believers such as Abel, Enoch, and Noah were also exam-

ples of faith; but Abraham manifested a unique pattern and became
the prototype for people of faith in all eras.

ABRAHAM'S PILGRIMAGE BY FAITH

When God first called Abraham, the future patriarch of the Jews lived
in Ur of Chaldea (Gen. 11:31; 15:7), a pagan, ignorant, idolatrous city
of perhaps 300,000 residents. Ur was a key center of commerce on
the lower Euphrates River in the region of Mesopotamia, just north-
west of the Persian Gulf.

The city was also a center of ancient culture and learning whose
citizens were proficient in various academic disciplines and skilled
trades. However, spiritually and religiously they were polytheis-
tic—they worshiped many gods. Therefore, Abraham was reared in
a pagan culture and family, since his father, Terah, was an idol worshiper (Josh. 24:2).

It was never Abraham's plan to leave Ur, then Haran, and eventually arrive in faraway Canaan. But God sovereignly revealed His
will to Abraham and called him from Ur. Only He knew what was
in store for Abraham. According to the writer of Hebrews 11:8, "By
faith Abraham, when he was called, obeyed by going out to a place
which he was to receive for an inheritance; and he went out, not
knowing where he was going." The Greek for "when he was called"
could also be translated "when he was being called," which indicates
that, remarkably, as soon as Abraham understood God's command
(Gen. 12:1), he obeyed and began the monumental disruption of life
that would follow. Final preparations for the long and demanding
journey could have taken days, weeks, or even months, but in
Abraham's mind he was already on his way, by faith, to wherever God
was leading him.

After God commanded Abraham to leave Ur for a new homeland, He promised to bless him, make him into a great nation, and
bless all other peoples on earth through him: "I will make you a great
nation, and I will bless you, and make your name great; and so you
shall be a blessing; and I will bless those who bless you, and the one

who curses you I will curse. And in you all the families of the earth shall be blessed" (Gen. 12:2-3). Armed with those two assurances, guaranteed solely by God's word, Abraham left the temporal security of his homeland for the future uncertainty of a long journey to a new land. He probably had only a remote idea of where Canaan was, and possibly had not heard of it at all. His future was surely a mystery to him. But his heart had been divinely moved so that he trusted the God who had called him.

After reaching Shechem in Canaan, Abraham received another unconditional promise from God: "The LORD appeared to Abram [Abraham] and said, 'To your descendants I will give this land.' So he built an altar there to the LORD who had appeared to him" (Gen. 12:7). As he went on toward Bethel and Ai, Abraham built another altar "and called upon the name of the LORD" (v. 8).

As great as Abraham's initial acts of faith were, he had some lapses and did not perfectly trust in the Lord during his early pilgrimage. For instance, he did not stay in Canaan and trust God during a famine. Instead, he sought help in Egypt and thereby placed himself and his wife Sarah in a compromising position with the pharaoh and ultimately with God. Abraham feared that the pharaoh would try to kill him and steal Sarah, so he deceitfully called Sarah his sister, thus dishonoring God and bringing plagues on the pharaoh's family (see Gen. 12:10-17).

Abraham also failed a test of his faith concerning the identity of his heir. Because of Sarah's barrenness, he followed his aging and childless wife's foolish advice and committed adultery with her maid, Hagar, in an effort to ensure that God's promise of descendants would be fulfilled. Abraham's disobedience again produced immense negative consequences. This brought grief to Hagar and to Ishmael, the son she bore by Abraham (see Gen. 16). It also brought future affliction and strife between Abraham's descendants and Ishmael's Arab descendants—troubles that continue to this very hour.

Despite his major lapses, Abraham's faith always remained with the Lord, who honored his perseverance with renewed promises and blessings. Sarah miraculously bore the promised son, Isaac, who soon became the focal point of Abraham's greatest test: "Now it came about after these things, that God tested Abraham, and said to him, 'Abraham!' And he said, 'Here I am.' And He said, 'Take now your son, your only son, whom you love, Isaac, and go to the land of Moriah; and offer him there as a burnt offering on one of the mountains of which I will tell you'" (Gen. 22:1-2).

At that time his faith did not waver, but he immediately began to obey God's command to offer Isaac as a sacrifice. God honored his faithfulness by sparing Isaac and providing a substitute sacrifice (Gen. 22:11-13). "By faith Abraham, when he was tested, offered up Isaac; and he who had received the promises was offering up his only begotten son; it was he to whom it was said, 'In Isaac your descendants shall be called.' He [Abraham] considered that God is able to raise men even from the dead; from which he also received him back as a type" (Heb. 11:17-19).

As a pilgrim or transient in Canaan (Heb. 11:9), Abraham had to be patient. (He probably also had to be patient while staying in Haran, even though he was not waiting to possess that land.) Therefore, Abraham had to exercise, to some degree, patience and faith for the rest of his life as he traversed the land God had promised. The great challenge for Abraham was that Canaan was constantly in sight but never in hand. In fact, none of the great patriarchs— Abraham, his son Isaac, his grandson Jacob—would ever physically possess the Promised Land. But the Holy Spirit enabled Abraham to respond obediently and patiently to God, by faith. Abraham waited patiently many long years for a promised son, who was finally given, and for a land, which was never given in his lifetime. (His descendants did not even possess Canaan until more than 500 years after it was first promised.)

The strength for Abraham's patience was his belief that God is faithful and his ultimate hope that his true inheritance was in heaven (Heb. 11:10).

ABRAHAM'S JUSTIFICATION BY FAITH

In spite of his sinfulness, but as a result of Abraham's persevering faith during his pilgrimage, God graciously declared him to be righteous, granting him forgiveness for all his sins. In that sense he is "the father of all who believe" (Rom. 4:11). The apostle Paul, quoting Genesis 15:6, further elaborated, "For what does the Scripture say? 'And Abraham believed God, and it was reckoned to him as righteousness.' Now to the one who works, his wage is not reckoned as a favor but as what is due. But to the one who does not work, but believes in Him who justifies the ungodly, his faith is reckoned as righteousness" (Rom. 4:3-5; cf. Gal. 3:6-7).

"Reckoned" is translated from the Greek *logizomai*, which had the economic and legal meaning of crediting something to another's account. The Lord, by His sovereign grace and mercy, credited Abraham's imperfect faith as righteousness in his spiritual account. God accepted his faith only because He chose to count it as righteousness.

Faith in Him is the only means God has ever provided for people to be justified. Faith itself is never the ground for anyone's justification, the death of Christ is. Faith is simply the channel through which God applies His saving grace. This is true not only for Abraham, but for everyone who has genuine faith: "Now to the one who works, his wage is not reckoned as a favor but as what is due. But to the one who does not work, but believes in Him who justifies the ungodly, his faith is reckoned as righteousness" (Rom. 4:4-5). And even that faith is a gift from God (Eph. 2:8-9).

Not by Circumcision

In Romans 4:9-12 the apostle Paul anticipated questions from the Jews about the role of circumcision in Abraham's justification:

> *Is this blessing then upon the circumcised, or upon the uncircumcised also? For we say, "Faith was reckoned to Abraham as righteousness." How then was it reckoned? While he was circumcised,*

> *or uncircumcised? Not while circumcised, but while uncircum-*
> *cised; and he received the sign of circumcision, a seal of the righ-*
> *teousness of the faith which he had while uncircumcised, that he*
> *might be the father of all who believe without being circumcised,*
> *that righteousness might be reckoned to them, and the father of cir-*
> *cumcision to those who not only are of the circumcision, but who*
> *also follow in the steps of the faith of our father Abraham which*
> *he had while uncircumcised.*

The chronology of Genesis further proves that Abraham was not justified by the act of circumcision. Abraham was ninety-nine years old and Ishmael thirteen when Abraham was circumcised (Gen. 17:23-25). But when God declared Abraham righteous (15:6), Ishmael was not even conceived yet (16:2-4). Abraham was eighty-six when Ishmael was born (16:16). So Abraham was justified at least fourteen years before his circumcision. In addition, Abraham was first given the covenant promise when he was seventy-five (Gen. 12:1-4), which means he was circumcised twenty-four years after he first entered a relationship of faith with the Lord.

Circumcision became the sign and seal of the covenant relationship between God and His people (Gen. 17:10-14), but it was never the basis for that covenant. It was a *sign* (physical surgery to remove the male foreskin and thus prevent disease being more readily passed from husband to wife) that pointed to the need for cleansing spiritually. It was designed to mark the Jews as the people of God's covenant promises. It was meant to make people aware that God wanted to circumcise their sinful hearts, not just their bodies. They needed cleansing of their souls. God provided that cleansing through their faith.

Anyone who trusts in physical circumcision, or any other such work or ceremony, in order to be made right with God places himself under the law's impossible demands and voids Christ's sacrificial death on his behalf. "For in Christ Jesus neither circumcision nor uncircumcision means anything, but faith working through love" (Gal. 5:6). So circumcision was a symbol, an illustration of what the heart required–cleansing, being made righteous by God through faith in Him and His Word.

Not by the Law

The Old Testament chronology also demonstrates that Abraham was not justified by keeping the Mosaic law. The law was not given to Moses (Exodus 20) until more than 500 years after Abraham lived; therefore the patriarch could not have been aware of the law's requirements.

Paul supplies the following concise theological exposition to further prove the law's inability to make Abraham or any other person righteous before God: "For the promise to Abraham or to his descendants that he would be heir of the world was not through the Law, but through the righteousness of faith. For if those who are of the Law are heirs, faith is made void and the promise is nullified; for the Law brings about wrath, but where there is no law, neither is there violation" (Rom. 4:13-15).

The promise again refers to God's covenant with Abraham, in which his family would be heirs of the world (see Gen. 12:3; 15:5-6; 18:18; 22:18). This promise contains four important elements.

It involves *a land* (Gen. 15:18-21) where Abraham would reside but not take possession. The land would first be conquered more than 500 years later by the Israelites under Joshua.

It involves *a people* who would be too numerous to count, like the dust of the earth and the stars of the sky (Gen. 13:16; 15:5). It fulfilled the statement that Abraham would be "the father of a multitude of nations" (Gen. 17:5; cf. Rom. 4:17).

The promise contains *a blessing* of the entire world through the patriarch's descendants (Gen. 12:3).

Finally, the promise is fulfilled in *a Redeemer*, one of Abraham's descendants who would bless the entire world through the provision of salvation. Abraham essentially heard the Gospel in this promise, as Paul explained to the Galatians: "And the Scripture, foreseeing that God would justify the Gentiles by faith, preached the gospel beforehand to Abraham, saying, 'All the nations shall be blessed in you'"

(Gal. 3:8). Even when God commanded that Isaac, the only heir, be sacrificed, Abraham believed the Gospel and trusted that the Lord would "provide for Himself the lamb for the burnt offering" (Gen. 22:8; cf. Heb. 11:17-19).

Later in Galatians 3 Paul further unfolds how the promise to Abraham blesses everyone in the world who believes: "The promises were spoken to Abraham and to his seed. He does not say, 'And to seeds,' as referring to many, but rather to one, 'And to your seed,' that is, Christ. . . . If you belong to Christ, then you are Abraham's offspring, heirs according to promise" (vv. 16, 29). Following Abraham's example of faith is thus being a kind of spiritual descendant, an heir with the Lord Jesus along with the patriarch. Mere physical descent from Abraham, if not combined with genuine faith and repentance, has no advantage at all, as Jesus plainly told the Jewish leaders (John 8:33-47).

ABRAHAM'S FAITH ANALYZED AND APPLIED

In Romans 4:18-25 the apostle Paul summarizes his illustration of Abraham as the spiritual prototype of every genuine believer and the foremost Old Testament example of saving faith:

> *In hope against hope he believed, in order that he might become a father of many nations, according to that which had been spoken, "So shall your descendants be." And without becoming weak in faith he contemplated his own body, now as good as dead since he was about a hundred years old, and the deadness of Sarah's womb; yet, with respect to the promise of God, he did not waver in unbelief, but grew strong in faith, giving glory to God, and being fully assured that what He had promised, He was able also to perform. Therefore also it was reckoned to him as righteousness. Now not for his sake only was it written, that "it was reckoned to him," but for our sake also, to whom it will be reckoned, as those who believe in Him who raised Jesus our Lord from the dead, He who was delivered up*

because of our transgressions, and was raised because of our justification.

This passage provides six important features of Abraham's faith and all God-given faith, the only kind that saves.

First, it says, "in hope against hope he [Abraham] believed." Hope and faith are distinguished in that hope is generally a confidence that something *will* happen, whereas faith is the confident conviction that something *has* happened. Abraham possessed hope when, humanly speaking, there was no basis for it. In the face of obstacles that seemed impossible to overcome, he trusted God to fulfill His word. Thus the object of his faith was God, as Genesis 15:5-6 confirms: "And He took him outside and said, 'Now look toward the heavens, and count the stars, if you are able to count them.' And He said to him, 'So shall your descendants be.' Then he believed in the LORD; and He reckoned it to him as righteousness."

Second, Abraham's faith in God did not weaken. When faith does weaken, it is often because we allow doubt to cloud and undermine it. However, for twenty-five years Abraham trusted God to give him an heir, and the patriarch continued to trust even when God tested him concerning Isaac (see again Heb. 11:17-19). The Genesis account does not say that prior to Isaac's birth Abraham had witnessed any miracles. But Abraham was convinced that the Lord could easily raise Isaac from the dead if such a miracle were necessary. Therefore he obeyed God through the most difficult of circumstances.

Third, because of his strong faith, Abraham was not discouraged by his own physical weakness and frailty. At age 100, Abraham's natural ability to procreate was gone; but that biological reality did not deter his faith in an all-powerful God who could work in spite of human deficiencies. Likewise, the fact that his wife Sarah was beyond her childbearing years did not keep Abraham from clinging to God's promises concerning Isaac (cf. Gen. 17:16, 21; 21:1-7).

Fourth, Abraham did not vacillate between faith and doubt, as we often do. Sarah, who "considered Him faithful who had promised" (Heb. 11:11), did not waver either, even though initially she was skeptical of God's promise to Abraham (Gen. 18:12).

Actually, some of the Genesis narratives seem to belie Paul's assertion in Romans 4:20 about Abraham's unwavering faith. For instance, Scripture says, "The word of the LORD came to Abram in a vision, saying, 'Do not fear, Abram, I am a shield to you; your reward shall be very great.' . . . Abram said, 'O LORD God, what wilt Thou give me, since I am childless, and the heir of my house is Eliezer of Damascus? . . . Since Thou hast given no offspring to me, one born in my house is my heir'" (Gen. 15:1-3). Abraham simply could not understand how, under the circumstances, God could fulfill His promise of a son who would produce many nations. (Eliezer, his chief servant, would have been Abraham's heir in place of a son born to Sarah.)

Just as temptation is not sin and does not necessarily result in sin, struggling faith is not doubt and does not inevitably lead to unbelief (cf. 2 Tim. 2:13). That Abraham was wrestling with God's plan signifies he was seeking to understand how it would unfold, although for the time being he was puzzled. Such sincere struggling comes from a godly faith that refuses to fall into the doubt and skepticism of a weaker faith. Undoubtedly God at times tested Abraham's faith (e.g., Gen. 22) in order to strengthen his trust, even as He does with our faith (see Jas. 1:2-4). To claim to grasp all of God's truth and see everything He is about to do stretches solid faith into proud presumption. Abraham "grew strong in faith" because the Lord had tested him.

Fifth, Abraham's faith glorified God. He gave all the credit to the One who bestowed true faith on him. This is yet another proof that Abraham's faith was genuine. In this way he exemplified the wonderful truth that faith in God, because it affirms His trustworthy character, is the greatest way men glorify Him. Any other kind of effort to worship the Lord is worthless and hypocritical and demonstrates that one is not trusting the God of Abraham (cf. 1 John 5:10).

Finally, Romans 4:21 summarizes the fact that Abraham's faith in God was complete and unqualified: "and being fully assured that what He had promised, He was able also to perform."

The account of Abraham and his faith is relevant for people today because the truth of justification applies to everyone who believes in Christ for salvation. The Holy Spirit made sure this truth was recorded for our sakes: "Now not for his [Abraham's] sake only was it written, that 'it was reckoned to him,' but for our sake also, to whom it will be reckoned, as those who believe in Him who raised Jesus our Lord from the dead" (Rom. 4:23-24; cf. 15:4; Ps. 78:5-7).

Even though Abraham had limited divine revelation (there was no written Scripture for centuries after his lifetime), Jesus asserted to the Jewish leaders that "Abraham rejoiced to see My day; and he saw it, and was glad" (John 8:56).

Abraham began his life as a pagan, idolatrous sinner. Though given limited revelation he laid aside his own works and trusted in the true and living God and His gracious promise of blessing and eternal life. He was thereby declared righteous. Men and women today, who have God's complete revelation available, have no excuse for not following Abraham's pattern of faith.

3

MOSES:

A LIFE OF

GODLY CHOICES

Godly living involves choosing to do what's right and necessary day after day. A believer's level of maturity and sanctification can usually be measured by the kinds of right and wrong choices he makes. He can make time for study of Scripture and prayer, or he can neglect them. In the workplace, the Christian must decide between making more money and attaining greater prestige at the expense of family and ministry, or devoting priority time and effort to the ministry and family.

Moses, better than many other biblical figures, understood how to make godly choices and right decisions. He knew how because even though he lived most of his life prior to receiving God's written law, he believed in the true God and lived accordingly.

Because of the events at Mt. Sinai (Exod. 20-40; cf. Deut. 4-30), Moses has always been associated with the law of God, to the extent that God's written law is commonly called the Mosaic law. Orthodox Judaism carries that association to its fullest extent by linking Moses to all of the commandments, rituals, and ceremonies of the Old Testament. But Moses, one of the most highly respected figures in the Hebrew Scripture, was not a legalist—he was a man of faith. And he is one of the greatest examples of how to exercise one's faith by consistently choosing God's way over the world's.

MOSES' PARENTS BELIEVE GOD'S PLANS

To curtail an amazing population increase among the Israelite slaves in Egypt, the pharaoh ordered all Hebrew homes searched and the baby boys of the Jews to be drowned in the Nile River (see Exod. 1:8-22). But Moses' parents, Amram and Jochebed, ignored the ruler's troubling decree because they knew it violated God's will. They protected their baby son first by hiding him and then by placing him in the Nile in a waterproofed basket at a location where he'd likely be found. Pharaoh's daughter found young Moses during one of her regular bathing times and adopted him as her own son.

God's providence further favored Moses when his watching sister Miriam persuaded the princess to have one of the Israelite women nurse the boy. Miriam was allowed to select her mother, who was able to care for her son Moses as if he had remained at home.

Moses' parents' concern extended beyond the fact that "he was a beautiful child" (Heb. 11:23). In Acts 7:20 Stephen told the Sanhedrin, "Moses . . . was lovely in the sight of God." Moses' mother and father were apparently aware of God's favor on their son. Thus they opposed the king's directive and did whatever they could, regardless of the consequences, to protect and save their son. We can't know exactly how much they knew about God's plan for Moses, but apparently they knew enough to realize that the Lord wanted to spare him for special usefulness.

Moses' mother, Jochebed, not only nursed him, but also taught him the Lord's promises to Israel—that the chosen people would inherit the Promised Land and become a great nation through which God would bless all other peoples (Gen. 12:1-3). She also imparted to him the messianic hope that originated in Genesis 3:15 and that Noah and Abraham had looked toward. Those promises and other great truths of God instilled in Moses the strong faith that would characterize his entire life.

What Moses' parents did for him required much confidence in God by them, especially that he would ultimately be reared according to God's will and not in the pagan religious teachings of Egypt.

They did not fully understand why God had allowed Moses to be taken to the very royal household that wanted all Israelite baby boys killed, but they faithfully trusted God for the results because they were convinced God is sovereign over all of life's events.

Amram and Jochebed's faith was later vindicated in the decisions Moses made after he was an adult in Egypt. He chose to reject the world's influences and instead by faith allowed the Lord to mold him into a godly leader who could guide the Israelites out of Egypt to Canaan.

MOSES REJECTS WORLDLY PRESTIGE

Moses lived forty years as a prince in Egypt, the superpower nation of that day, a country that had a strong economy and a highly cultured society. In such an environment Moses had all the advantages any young man would ever want: "And Moses was educated in all the learning of the Egyptians, and he was a man of power in words and deeds" (Acts 7:22). He learned to read and write hieroglyphics, hieratic writing (an ancient Egyptian cursive that was simpler than hieroglyphics), and probably some Canaanite languages (as well as learning Hebrew from his mother).

In spite of all the years of influence from paganism in Egypt, however, Moses never faltered in his commitment to God or his hope in the promises for Israel. Therefore, when he became forty he was at a crossroad—he had to choose between the privileges of Egypt and loyal identification with his own people, Israel.

Moses' faith in the God of Israel and his resolve to make the right choices determined which way he would go: "By faith Moses, when he had grown up, refused to be called the son of Pharaoh's daughter" (Heb. 11:24). Furthermore, we see from Stephen's sermon to the Sanhedrin that God had revealed to Moses his special role of service and ministry to Israel: "He supposed that his brethren understood that God was granting them deliverance through him; but they did not understand" (Acts 7:25). The Israelites may not have understood Moses' mission, but he did; and he also realized that for the remainder of his life he was to be exclusively one of God's chosen leaders for his fellow Jews.

During his time in Egypt, the circumstances of Moses and his fellow Israelites were reminiscent of those faced by Joseph and Israel in Egypt, but with some important differences. Joseph, who served as prime minister in Egypt, used that nation's power to help God's people, who were shepherds and farmers in the land and were honored by the pharaoh. Moses, by contrast, had to oppose Egyptian might in order to deliver the Israelites from slavery and lead them into the Promised Land.

The world says Moses sacrificed everything for nothing. But believers know he sacrificed nothing for everything. He renounced the world's fleeting prestige for the sake of God's permanent blessings and rewards (cf. Heb. 11:26). God honors people by an entirely different set of criteria from what the world uses. He is not as interested in prominent family heritage, great wealth, high education, or business success as He is in faith that completely rests on Him and demonstrates itself in sacrificial service.

C. T. Studd, the famous nineteenth-century English cricketer-turned-missionary, is another example of a man who was willing to repudiate wealth and worldly acclaim in favor of the kingdom of God. The upper-class cricket fans of English society in the 1880s were astounded when Studd, "the most brilliant member of a well-known cricketing family," turned his back on fame and luxury to become a missionary to China. John Pollock writes the following about Studd and the influence his brothers had on him not long after they were all converted:

> The boys went to Cambridge University and captained the Cambridge cricket eleven one after another. But while George and Kynaston gave a strong witness to the love of Christ, C. T. (as he was known) "was selfish and kept the knowledge all to myself. The result was that my love began to grow cold, the love of the world came in."

In the autumn of 1882 Kynaston Studd organized D. L. Moody's great mission to Cambridge, but C. T. was away in Australia with the English cricket team, recovering "The Ashes." When he returned, he continued his cricketing triumphs. He was tall, good looking, with black, wavy hair and a pleasant manner, but as a Christian witness he was a nonentity. Then, in November 1883, his brother George fell desperately ill and was believed to be dying. Keeping watch by the bedside in their London home, C. T. began to realize how seduced he had been by the honor, riches and pleasures of the world. "All these things had become as nothing to my brother. He only cared about the Bible and the Lord Jesus Christ; and God taught me the same lesson." ("Cricketing Missionary: C. T. Studd," in *More Than Conquerors*, edited by John Woodbridge [Chicago: Moody Press, 1992], 217)

MOSES REJECTS THE WORLD'S PLEASURES AND WEALTH

Living in the royal palace, Moses had all the earthly advantages he could have wanted—the best food, living quarters, recreational facilities, scholarly resources, and everything else his era could provide. Twentieth-century archaeological discoveries such as the treasures of Tutankhamen's (King Tut's) tomb prove how wealthy Egypt was in its heyday. (Tutankhamen lived just a century or so after Moses.)

Those material comforts were not sinful per se. Decades earlier Joseph had enjoyed the same things in the same place as he finished his career serving Pharaoh while still remaining obedient to the Lord. But it would have been a sin for Moses to follow the same course because he knew God was calling him to leave the palace and serve the people of Israel. Thus Moses faced a choice: he could obey God's call or disobey and enjoy the comforts of the royal court. He knew that no matter how intensely satisfying they can be temporarily, the world's pleasures are deceptive and fleeting. And so often they are entangled with sin, which cannot bring good to us or others or glory to God. Moses realized that truth as well as any follower of God and made a conscious choice, by faith, to "endure ill-treatment with the people of God, [rather] than to enjoy the passing pleasures of sin" (Heb. 11:25).

Moses was confident that if he obeyed God's will even when it became difficult, he ultimately would be blessed. That principle of faith and obedience is true for all believers. God wants His children to depart from sin and pursue sanctification. This process is not always easy, but the positive results are far preferable to the negative consequences of sin.

The author of Hebrews further analyzes how and why Moses rejected the attractions of the world: "considering the reproach of Christ greater riches than the treasures of Egypt; for he was looking to the reward" (11:26). Moses carefully weighed the pros and cons of his decision (the Greek word translated "considering" denotes conscientious, prudent thinking rather than impulsive decision-making). His final choice was well-founded and certain, because he knew God's way was far superior to anything Egypt could offer.

It's noteworthy that verse 26 refers to an aspect of Moses' relationship to Christ even though he lived 1,500 years before His coming. *Christ* means "messiah" or "anointed one" and was often used for Old Testament people who were set apart for special service to God. Therefore it's possible that Moses viewed himself as some kind of messiah or deliverer, or more theologically, as a formal type of Christ (just as Joseph and Joshua are types of Christ).

But I believe the writer of Hebrews was referring to Jesus Christ Himself. Therefore, Moses suffered reproach for Christ because he identified with the true Messiah's people long before He came to earth. Salvation has always been by grace through faith, which means any believer who has ever suffered for God, as Moses did, has also suffered for Jesus Christ (see Ps. 69:9; Gal. 6:17). In Scripture, Messiah has always been identified closely with His people (e.g., compare Hos. 11:1 with Matt. 2:15). Therefore, when the Israelites suffered as slaves in Egypt, Messiah suffered; and when Moses suffered, Christ suffered.

Scripture does not reveal exactly how much Moses knew about God's Son, the future Redeemer. But since Moses had significantly more divine revelation than Abraham, it is safe to assert that Moses looked forward to the Redeemer as much as that patriarch did (cf. John 8:56).

MOSES REJECTS WORLDLY INTIMIDATION

The Bible text does not say so, but Moses probably dreaded the prospect of living in the desert when he first fled Egypt (Exod. 2:15). One thing is certain—itinerant, nomadic, desert living would be a huge step down from the luxuries of the royal court. Moses could not have imagined that he would soon marry the shepherdess Zipporah and tend her father Reuel's flock for the next forty years.

The biggest intimidation Moses had to deal with, however, was fear. But he did not give in to it when the Lord called him out of Egypt. Moses was sustained by his strong and persistent faith in God's guidance, "for he endured, as seeing Him who is unseen" (Heb. 11:27). In overcoming his fears, Moses could agree with David's words in Psalm 27:1, "The LORD is my light and my salvation; whom shall I fear? The LORD is the defense of my life; whom shall I dread?"

When Moses departed Egypt the second time (forty years later) and led all the Israelites on the journey to the Promised Land, he encountered resistance not only from the pharaoh but from the people of Israel (cf. Exod. 6:9; 14:11-12). However, he was not intimidated by either. Instead, he fearlessly continued to be God's spokesman and to do His will.

MOSES ACCEPTS GOD'S PROVISION AND PROMISE

After accepting the Lord's plan and call for his life and rejecting the allurements and oppositions from the world, Moses needed to accept God's provision of salvation and His promise of victory. Moses was faithful and obedient in both ways, as Hebrews again summarizes: "By faith he kept the Passover and the sprinkling of the blood, so that he who destroyed the first-born might not touch them [Moses and the Israelites]. By faith they passed through the Red Sea as though they were passing through dry land; and the Egyptians, when they attempted it, were drowned" (11:28-29).

The last of the ten plagues God sent against the land of Egypt required the death of all firstborn, both humans and animals (Exod. 11:5). The Lord instituted the Passover to spare the Jews from the fatal consequences of that plague. He commanded them to sprinkle lamb's blood on the doorposts and lintels of their houses (12:7) so the angel who carried out the plague would pass over all the Israelites' homes.

Moses and the people did not grasp all the ramifications of the first Passover, but they knew it was part of God's plan, and so they obeyed. The sprinkled lamb's blood was symbolic and predictive of Christ's future work at Calvary by which He conquered death and atoned for all who believe in Him. Moses by faith accepted God's provision of salvation, an action that illustrates how all people are to respond to God's grace, even when that response is beyond complete human understanding.

Later, when Moses and the Israelites arrived at the Red Sea's shoreline, the people realized they were about to be trapped and killed by the pursuing Egyptian army. When Moses' countrymen saw there was no escape, they became anxious and were filled with bitter sarcasm toward him: "Is it because there were no graves in Egypt that you have taken us away to die in the wilderness?" (Exod. 14:11). But Moses rallied their spirits and directed their hearts and eyes toward God when he declared, "Do not fear! Stand by and see the salvation of the LORD which He will accomplish for you today. . . . The LORD will fight for you while you keep silent" (vv. 13-14).

The people then believed God's promise for deliverance, given through Moses, and proceeded forward on the pathway that emerged when the sea parted (Exod. 14:15-22). The Israelites had no guarantee except God's word that the walls of water would not come back together too soon and drown them all (as subsequently happened to the presumptuous Egyptian soldiers, vv. 23-28). But they and Moses exercised faith, and God preserved them (cf. vv. 29-31). For all who are faithful and obedient, God's word is always enough.

For forty years, Moses enjoyed the wealth and privileges of a high-ranking position in Egypt. However, he chose to leave them behind—"by faith he forsook Egypt" (Heb. 11:27, KJV)-because they were stumbling blocks to his obeying the Lord and being rewarded in eternity for his godly service. Likewise, all believers should be willing to abandon temporal pleasures and selfish indulgences and to sacrifice all for God's kingdom, being assured that the "momentary, light affliction is producing for us an eternal weight of glory far beyond all comparison" (2 Cor. 4:17; cf. Rom. 8:18).

4

RAHAB:

D I S T I N C T I V E

F A I T H

Rahab is an unlikely candidate for a book on great biblical characters who walked in the footsteps of faith. She was a Gentile prostitute, a member of the immoral Amorite race that God had marked for destruction (see Gen. 15:16). She was just an average citizen of Jericho, at the bottom of the socioeconomic scale. Yet Rahab is listed along with Noah, Abraham, Moses, and other more noble Old Testament personalities in the Hall of Fame of the Faithful (Heb. 11:31). As the great-grandmother of David (cf. Matt. 1:5), she also became an ancestor of Jesus. These last two facts make her a woman worthy of our consideration.

RAHAB MEETS THE TWO SPIES

Rahab first appears in Scripture in Joshua 2:1-5:

> *Then Joshua the son of Nun sent two men as spies secretly from Shittim, saying, "Go, view the land, especially Jericho." So they went and came into the house of a harlot whose name was Rahab, and lodged there. And it was told the king of Jericho, saying, "Behold, men from the sons of Israel have come here tonight to search out the land." And the king of Jericho sent word to Rahab, saying, "Bring out the men who have come to you,*

*who have entered your house, for they have come to search out
all the land." But the woman had taken the two men and hidden them, and she said, "Yes, the men came to me, but I did not
know where they were from. And it came about that when it was
time to shut the gate, at dark, that the men went out; I do not
know where the men went. Pursue them quickly, for you will
overtake them."*

Following Moses' death and the Israelites' forty-year stay in the
desert wilderness after their exodus from Egypt, it was finally time for
them to enter the Promised Land. Joshua, who had succeeded Moses
as commander-in-chief, was taking all the precautions any skillful
general would use when moving into new territory. Accordingly, he
sent two spies to reconnoiter the eastern border of Canaan, particularly the border city of Jericho that was right on the banks of the
Jordan River.

Joshua sent the men secretly so that even the children of Israel,
much less the Canaanites, would not know what he was doing. He
wanted to avoid any furor of a frightened debate among the people
about the wisdom of sending spies into the land. It is likely the spies
began their covert operation at night. They first had to swim the
Jordan in the dark, then approach the strongly fortified city of Jericho,
enter the city gate, and find a place to stay from which they could
assess the city's defenses.

The lodging the men chose turned out to be a prostitute's house.
They did not choose the place for immoral reasons (it's safe to
assume they did not even know it was a house of prostitution). They
chose it in order to be less conspicuous while they were learning what
they could about the city. And because the house was located along
the city wall, it afforded them the opportunity for a quick getaway if
necessary. Also, God in His sovereign providence wanted them there
because Rahab had a heart ready to receive His saving truth.

But the scouts were novice spies, and their presence was soon
discovered (vv. 2-3). Jericho's city king, who was more like a mayor
with military control, was obviously frightened over any potential

invasion from the massive encampment of Israelites across the Jordan. The history of Israel's miraculous escape from Egypt and her wilderness wanderings was somewhat common knowledge to the people of the region, and therefore the king was fearful of Israel's next potential move and was desperate to maintain his power in Jericho.

RAHAB HELPS THE SPIES

The spies and their covert operation were in jeopardy, but the faith-filled Rahab came to their rescue. Before the king's messengers arrived, she remained true to the laws of Middle Eastern hospitality and risked her life to secure her guests: "But the woman had taken the two men and hidden them" (v. 4). And after the officials reached her house, Rahab further protected the spies by lying about their location (v. 5).

It was not right for Rahab to lie about where the Israelite spies were. Even though her heart was open to God's saving truth, her knowledge of Him was extremely limited. She was a victim of her own fallen nature, and her ethics were those of the corrupt Canaanite culture. She did not understand the value God puts on truth. He honored her faith, as we will see, but her lie was unnecessary. No lie provides any assistance to God. He needs no help, especially sinful efforts.

Rahab also would have been unaware of the sinfulness of lying because the laws of Eastern hospitality surpassed the laws of honesty. Honoring and protecting your guests was the greatest moral imperative. When someone was sheltered in your home, even your greatest enemy, you were bound to save his or her life if you could.

Therefore, it was not God's will that Rahab lie to rescue the scouts—He could have and would have saved them anyway. But she did so, and none of us will know what providential means or miraculous methods God might have used to preserve the two men otherwise. Joshua 2:6 reveals the first part of what actually happened: "But she had brought them [the spies] up to the roof and hidden them in the stalks of flax which she had laid in order on the roof."

Since it was harvesttime, the spies could have easily hidden behind the three- to four-feet-high flax bundles on the roof of Rahab's house. That allowed time for the king's messengers to be diverted out of the city, toward the two or three fords of the Jordan: "I do not know where the men went. Pursue them quickly, for you will overtake them. . . . So the men pursued them on the road to the Jordan to the fords; and as soon as those who were pursuing them had gone out, they shut the gate" (2:5, 7).

RAHAB'S PLEDGE OF FAITH

Rahab then made clear to the two Israelites why she was intervening on their behalf:

> *Now before they lay down, she came up to them on the roof, and said to the men, "I know that the LORD has given you the land, and that the terror of you has fallen on us, and that all the inhabitants of the land have melted away before you. For we have heard how the LORD dried up the water of the Red Sea before you when you came out of Egypt, and what you did to the two kings of the Amorites who were beyond the Jordan, to Sihon and Og, whom you utterly destroyed. And when we heard it, our hearts melted and no courage remained in any man any longer because of you; for the LORD your God, He is God in heaven above and on earth beneath. Now therefore, please swear to me by the LORD, since I have dealt kindly with you, that you also will deal kindly with my father's household, and give me a pledge of truth, and spare my father and my mother and my brothers and my sisters, with all who belong to them, and deliver our lives from death." So the men said to her, "Our life for yours if you do not tell this business of ours; and it shall come about when the LORD gives us the land that we will deal kindly and faithfully with you."*
> —*Josh.* 2:8-14

Amazingly, God's promise to Israel had somehow become known to Rahab, likely because Israel's exploits were already widely reported and feared in that region. But Rahab demonstrated faith as well as fear—surprisingly strong faith in the true God. She was so sure of the Lord's supremacy and power that she sought to make a solemn pledge with the spies, to which they agreed (vv. 12-14). Rahab then helped the men get out her back window and directed them on their way (vv. 15-16). However, they didn't depart without adding one more significant stipulation to the pledge: "And the men said to her, 'We shall be free from this oath to you which you have made us swear, unless, when we come into the land, you tie this cord of scarlet thread in the window through which you let us down, and gather to yourself into the house your father and your mother and your brothers and all your father's household'" (vv. 17-18).

Nearly all faithful commentators of the Old Testament interpret the scarlet cord as a symbol of the blood of Christ, connecting it to His future death on the cross. But we also must look backward from the scarlet cord to the Passover, when God sent the angel of death to kill all the firstborn and spared only those Israelites whose doorposts were marked with lamb's blood (Exod. 11:1-12:28). That blood was symbolic of the coming Savior whose shed blood would save all sinners who believe in Him. The scarlet cord that Rahab obediently placed in her window as a sign of her faith (Josh. 2:21) is therefore another analogy to the shed blood of Jesus Christ.

RAHAB'S FAITH VINDICATED

The wonderful conclusion to the story of Rahab occurs in Joshua 6:22-25, immediately after the destruction of Jericho (6:15-21):

> *And Joshua said to the two men who had spied out the land, "Go into the harlot's house and bring the woman and all she has out of there, as you have sworn to her." So the young men who were spies went in and brought out Rahab and her father and her mother and her brothers and all she had; they also brought out all her relatives, and placed them outside the camp of Israel. And they*

> *burned the city with fire, and all that was in it. Only the silver*
> *and gold and articles of bronze and iron, they put into the treasury*
> *of the house of the LORD. However, Rahab the harlot and her*
> *father's household and all she had, Joshua spared; and she has*
> *lived in the midst of Israel to this day, for she hid the messengers*
> *whom Joshua sent to spy out Jericho.*

Though an unlovely woman, Rahab is a lovely example of saving faith. She was a prostitute in a pagan city who had none of the spiritual advantages of the Israelites, and certainly none of the things we take for granted (the Bible, good preaching and teaching, worship services, Christian radio and literature). Yet, in spite of all her disadvantages, she was like a beautiful pearl lying within a rough, drab oyster shell on the ocean bottom among the rocks and weeds. God could see through the debris of sin to her true, heartfelt faith, and He drew her to Himself. That caused her to accept His warnings, fear His judgment, desire to be spared by His mercy, and willingly act in simple obedience (by hanging a red cord out her window to identify her house). Rahab's model of faith is best summarized by her affirmations in Joshua 2:9, 11: "I know that the LORD has given you the land . . . for the LORD your God, He is God in heaven above and on earth beneath."

The remarkable and encouraging message found in Rahab's story is that God judges impenitent sinners but spares those who believe in Him. Her type of lifestyle (prostitution), along with all the other evils in the pagan city of Jericho, resulted in God's judgment. Yet Rahab escaped divine wrath because she was a sinner who believed in the true God. What distinguished her from the other people in Jericho was not her superior morality or greater number of good deeds. Nor was it higher intelligence or a better disposition. It was simply her faith.

Rahab's faith was fully demonstrated when she risked all to help the two spies from Israel. (She undoubtedly would have been killed as a traitor had the king's messengers discovered she was sheltering enemy spies.) She entrusted everything to the Lord and proved she was completely committed to Him, no matter what the cost. Rahab, without knowing Jesus' teaching on discipleship (cf. Mark 8:34), was willing to obey God no matter how difficult the situation. And that's how it should be for us who follow Christ today. Our inner life of faith ought to be reflected in an outward life of faithfulness and good works.

5

HANNAH:

THE FAITHFUL

MOTHER

Motherhood is the highest calling God will ever give to a Christian woman. It is not, however, the only proper role a woman can fulfill. Sometimes it is God's will for women to remain single (cf. 1 Cor. 7:8-9) or for some who are married to stay childless. But it has been God's plan from the beginning for most women to rear godly children (cf. 1 Tim. 5:10; Titus 2:3-5). An early illustration of that plan is Sarah, who is a model of faith and obedience in marriage and motherhood. There is also the example of Rachel, whom the Lord allowed to die after giving birth to Benjamin (Gen. 35:16-20). Ruth was the epitome of love and sacrifice and was also blessed to be the mother of Obed, an ancestor of the Lord Jesus. Consider too the cousins Elizabeth and Mary, the mothers of John the Baptist and our Lord respectively.

We find the most scriptural detail concerning a faithful mother, however, when we study the life of Hannah. Her name denotes grace and beauty, which is what she displayed when God tested her faith and character before granting her a son.

Hannah first appears in 1 Samuel 1, toward the end of the difficult period of the judges in Israel. That was a time of moral and religious degeneracy and political confusion and distress. With the death of Samson, Israel was leaderless and vulnerable to her enemies, the Philistines. The nation needed a great leader and a great man, and

God needed a great woman to shape that man. Samuel was the man, and Hannah was the godly mother who, with God's help, influenced his character.

Hannah had three right relationships in her life that made her a godly wife and mother.

HANNAH'S RIGHT RELATIONSHIP WITH HER HUSBAND

We find the beginning of Hannah's story in 1 Samuel 1:1-2: "Now there was a certain man from Ramathaim-zophim from the hill country of Ephraim, and his name was Elkanah the son of Jeroham, the son of Elihu, the son of Tohu, the son of Zuph, an Ephraimite. And he had two wives: the name of one was Hannah and the name of the other Peninnah; and Peninnah had children, but Hannah had no children."

Hannah's marriage was obviously not a perfect one, because it was polygamous. Polygamy was a normal part of human culture in those ancient times and God was patient with that sin, but it was never God's design for marriage (Gen. 2:24) and always produced negative consequences. And Elkanah's having a second wife—probably to compensate for Hannah's barrenness, to produce children who could possess his inheritance—created a very difficult situation for Hannah.

Nonetheless, that marriage transcended the sin of polygamy, so that Hannah did have a right relationship with Elkanah. Several features indicate this fact.

Hannah Worshiped with Her Husband

First of all, Hannah and Elkanah worshiped God together: "Now this man [Elkanah] would go up from his city yearly to worship and to sacrifice to the LORD of hosts in Shiloh" (1 Sam. 1:3). "Yearly" doesn't mean that Elkanah and his family went to worship just once a year. It indicates that he attended such worship every year and probably went at least three times annually—to the Feast of Unleavened Bread, the Feast of Weeks, and the Feast of Booths (cf. Deut. 16:16-

17). Elkanah went to Shiloh because that was the place of worship before the Ark of the Covenant was relocated to Jerusalem.

So Hannah had a devout, God-fearing husband, which always makes any believing mother's responsibility for bringing up her children "in the discipline and instruction of the Lord" so much easier and more effective (Eph. 6:4; cf. 2 Cor. 6:14). Hannah knew she needed a husband who would provide spiritual leadership and would be an example of godliness through family worship. (See Deut. 7:3, Josh. 23:11-13, and Ezra 9:10-15 for God's commandments and warnings regarding marriage with unbelievers.)

Hannah and Elkanah Loved Each Other

Elkanah loved Hannah rather than Peninnah, and Scripture says he did not hide that fact: "And when the day came that Elkanah sacrificed, he would give portions to Peninnah his wife and to all her sons and her daughters; but to Hannah he would give a double portion, for he loved Hannah" (1 Sam. 1:4-5). This further illustrates that his relationship with Peninnah was merely pragmatic, for the sake of having heirs.

Peace offerings were part of the worship, and after the priest took his small portion, most of the offering was given back to the family for a feast. As the one who really had his heart and whom he loved, Hannah received a double portion from Elkanah for the family feast. His gesture was far more than an emotional response; it was a love of kindness, thoughtfulness, sacrifice, and honor. Like all wives, Hannah found her security in the kind of love that Elkanah publicly demonstrated to her at the feast.

Hannah Received Her Husband's Sympathy

Even though her husband Elkanah lovingly gave her a double portion at the worship feast, Hannah was not always able to enjoy the portion. Verses 6-9 provide a background explanation and also indicate how Elkanah further met her need: "Her rival [Peninnah], however, would provoke her bitterly to irritate her, because the LORD had closed her womb. And it happened year after year, as often as she went up to the house of the LORD, she would provoke her, so she wept and would not eat. Then Elkanah her husband said to her, 'Hannah, why do you weep and why do you not eat and why is your heart sad? Am I not better to you than ten sons?' Then Hannah rose after eating and drinking in Shiloh."

Hannah was truly blessed by her husband's response. Elkanah knew of the conflict between Hannah and Peninnah, that it was deliberately intensified by Peninnah, and that it was a deeply painful and difficult situation for Hannah. But he had a sympathetic heart and thoughtfully read Hannah's feelings. That enabled him not to pontificate but simply to ask a question that revealed his shared feelings and reassured her of his deep love.

HANNAH'S RIGHT RELATIONSHIP WITH GOD

Hannah, as she prepared by faith to be a godly mother, not only had a deep and right relationship with her husband, but also a right heavenly relationship. She fully realized that she had to take her problem of childlessness straight to the Lord. By responding in that way, Hannah displayed six godly virtues.

Hannah Had a Passion for the Lord's Best

Hannah had a compelling longing for the Lord's best in life, but what does that mean practically? Quite simply, she desperately wanted a child—so much so that she wept and fasted before God. But Hannah did not seek a child for selfish motives; she did not desire to show off a son in order to elevate her own status or to use him to fulfill her own need for love. She wanted the child to dedicate him to the Lord.

Hannah undoubtedly realized that children are an inheritance from the Lord (cf. Gen. 33:5). The psalmist later expressed it this way:

> *He makes the barren woman abide in the house as a joyful mother of children. Praise the LORD!*
> —113:9

*Behold, children are a gift of the LORD; the fruit of the womb is
a reward. Like arrows in the hand of a warrior, so are the children
of one's youth.*

—127:3-4

A truly godly woman like Hannah has the God-given heart of a
mother. She passionately longs to have a child because she sees children as gifts from God to be returned to Him, special blessings of His
love, and the fulfillment of His primary intention for women.

Hannah Was a Woman of Prayer

One of the most noble aspects of Hannah's godliness was that she
was a woman of prayer. Because she understood that God was the
source of children (see Ps. 139:13-16), she knew that He alone could
alter her sterility. The writer of 1 Samuel describes Hannah's diligence in prayer in the temple in this way: "And she, greatly distressed, prayed to the LORD and wept bitterly. And she made a vow
and said, 'O LORD of hosts, if Thou wilt indeed look on the affliction of Thy maidservant and remember me, and not forget Thy
maidservant, but wilt give Thy maidservant a son, then I will give
him to the LORD all the days of his life, and a razor shall never come
on his head'" (1:10-11).

Hannah slipped into God's sanctuary and poured out her heart
to Him in honest, open prayer. Constant, persevering faith was the
distinctive virtue of her praying, as verse 12 suggests: "she continued praying before the LORD." Thus Hannah exemplified the spirit
of all true prayer warriors; she stayed with it and did not quit, which
is exactly what the apostle Paul instructed believers to do centuries
later: "pray without ceasing" (1 Thess. 5:17; cf. Luke 18:1-8).

Hannah Was a Woman of Promise

Hannah further displayed the model character of the godly mother
by promising to present her son completely to the Lord: "And she
made a vow and said, 'O LORD of hosts, if Thou wilt indeed look on
the affliction of Thy maidservant and remember me, and not forget

Thy maidservant, but wilt give Thy maidservant a son, then I will give him to the LORD all the days of his life, and a razor shall never come on his head'" (1 Sam. 1:11).

The last part of her promise was a Nazirite vow (see Num. 6:4-8; Judg. 13:5; 16:7). If an Israelite man wanted to be totally consecrated to God, he would sometimes pledge to live an austere life, with no concern for fashionable clothing or stylish physical appearance. That necessarily included letting one's hair grow, avoiding the rich foods of banquets and celebrations, and abstaining from wine or strong drink. Many Jewish men took Nazirite vows for short periods, but Scripture records only three who were lifelong Nazirites: Samson, John the Baptist, and Hannah's son, Samuel.

So Hannah made a vow for the right reason and with the right attitude. If God granted her a son, she wanted to rear him as a godly man who would serve the Lord and glorify Him. In essence, she would give Samuel back to God. Since a married woman's vow could be confirmed or nullified by her husband, Elkanah must have agreed (cf. Num. 30:6-15).

Hannah Was a Pure Woman

Another godly virtue Hannah exhibited was purity. But others did not always recognize it, as, for example, when she continued her intense time of prayer in the temple:

> *Now it came about, as she continued praying before the LORD, that Eli was watching her mouth. As for Hannah, she was speaking in her heart, only her lips were moving, but her voice was not heard. So Eli thought she was drunk. Then Eli said to her, "How long will you make yourself drunk? Put away your wine from you." But Hannah answered and said, "No, my lord, I am a woman oppressed in spirit; I have drunk neither wine nor strong drink, but I have poured out my soul before the LORD. Do not consider your maidservant as a worthless woman; for I have spoken until now out of my great concern and provocation." Then Eli*

answered and said, "Go in peace; and may the God of Israel grant
your petition that you have asked of Him."
                                                   —*1 Sam. 1:12-17*

Eli, the high priest who observed Hannah as he sat near the door-post of the temple (v. 9), may have been observant, but he was not very discerning as to what was actually happening with Hannah. In fact, his lack of discernment here showed his incompetence as a high priest, as subsequent chapters of 1 Samuel clearly reveal.

Eli misinterpreted the silent movement of Hannah's lips as evidence of public drunkenness. She graciously but firmly denied his allegation (vv. 15-16). That denial and her clarifying assertion that she was actually praying during a time of "great concern and provocation" were in keeping with the kind of virtuous woman she was (cf. Prov. 12:4; 31:10).

Hannah's godly character also explains why she did not want to be considered "a worthless woman" (literally, "a daughter of Belial"). That was a common Old Testament expression for men or women who practiced idolatry (Deut. 13:12-15), were rebellious (1 Sam. 2:12-17), engaged in lewd and sensuous acts (Judg. 19-20), were arrogant and insensitive (1 Sam. 25:9-10, 25), and even committed murder (1 Kings 21:6-13). Hannah, although she undoubtedly would have humbly acknowledged her actual sins, knew she should not be characterized in such an evil manner.

Hannah Had Patient Faith
Hannah's final response to Eli reveals another of her positive spiritual traits: "And she said, 'Let your maidservant find favor in your sight.' So the woman went her way and ate, and her face was no longer sad" (1 Sam. 1:18). Hannah cast her heartfelt burden on God and refused to remain frustrated. That demonstrates genuine, patient faith. People with such faith don't pray, "O God, here's my problem" and then leave His presence in complete doubt and frustration. Instead they pray, "Here's my problem, God" and then leave it with Him, totally trusting the Lord to handle it. Believers with faith like Hannah's will cast

their heaviest burdens on God (1 Pet. 5:6-7) and will patiently go on with their lives, not allowing their deepest concerns to keep them sad.

Hannah Was a Woman of Praise

When God answered Hannah's prayer and gave her a son, her thankful soul responded with a pure, unbroken stream of praise. Her words, recorded for us in 1 Samuel 2:1-10, are a masterpiece of what genuine praise ought to include. This passage, much like Mary's *Magnificat* in Luke 1:46-55, is worth our careful attention and meditation:

> *My heart exults in the LORD; my horn is exalted in the LORD, my mouth speaks boldly against my enemies, because I rejoice in Thy salvation. There is no one holy like the LORD, indeed, there is no one besides Thee, nor is there any rock like our God. Boast no more so very proudly, do not let arrogance come out of your mouth; for the LORD is a God of knowledge, and with Him actions are weighed. The bows of the mighty are shattered, but the feeble gird on strength. Those who were full hire themselves out for bread, but those who were hungry cease to hunger. Even the barren gives birth to seven, but she who has many children languishes. The LORD kills and makes alive; He brings down to Sheol and raises up. The LORD makes poor and rich; He brings low, He also exalts. He raises the poor from the dust, He lifts the needy from the ash heap to make them sit with nobles, and inherit a seat of honor; for the pillars of the earth are the LORD's, and He set the world on them. He keeps the feet of His godly ones, but the wicked ones are silenced in darkness; for not by might shall a man prevail. Those who contend with the LORD will be shattered; against them He will thunder in the heavens, the LORD will judge the ends of the earth; and He will give strength to His king, and will exalt the horn of His anointed.*

HANNAH'S RIGHT RELATIONSHIP IN HER HOME

The third major character quality Hannah possessed was a faithfulness to her responsibilities at home. First, that involved a dedication to the new son God had given her (1 Sam. 1:19-20). The author of 1 Samuel goes on to say, "Then the man Elkanah went up with all his household to offer to the LORD the yearly sacrifice and pay his vow. But Hannah did not go up, for she said to her husband, 'I will not go up until the child is weaned; then I will bring him, that he may appear before the LORD and stay there forever.' And Elkanah her husband said to her, 'Do what seems best to you. Remain until you have weaned him; only may the LORD confirm His word.' So the woman remained and nursed her son until she weaned him" (vv. 21-23).

The round-trip journey by foot between Ramah and Shiloh would have taken Hannah's family two or three weeks. Such a long trip did not appeal to her at all because she was completely dedicated to the care of Samuel. She did not want to disrupt his gentle home routine and quiet nursing environment, or to make him uncomfortable during the long walk. That's a marked contrast to so many mothers today who have babies and several months later place them in day-care centers and hurry back to work.

Hannah was committed to staying at home to rear her son and to instruct him in the truths of God (cf. Deut. 6:6-9), preparing him for the time when she and her husband would give him to the Lord's service in the temple. Thus she was not only devoted to her child's welfare in the home, but she also wanted to dedicate him to God, just as she had promised.

Hannah sought nothing for Samuel that others could have viewed as prestigious for him or self-gratifying for her—no wealthy and successful career that she could brag about and then depend on later for financial support in her old age. She simply gave Samuel away to God: "Now when she had weaned him, she took him up with her, with a three-year-old bull and one ephah of flour and a jug of wine, and brought him to the house of the LORD in Shiloh, although the child was young. Then they slaughtered the bull, and brought the boy to Eli" (1 Sam. 1:24-25).

Hannah never really let go of her responsibility to Samuel (see 1 Sam. 2:18-19), and she was always faithful in her relationships with Elkanah and the Lord, and God honored that.

The hope for society rests on the next generation, and what that next generation will be like depends a great deal on the present actions of godly mothers. Hannah is certainly a role model of godly motherhood and an excellent example of one who walked in the footsteps of faith.

6

JONAH:

THE RELUCTANT

MISSIONARY

Scripture teaches that God chose Israel from the beginning to be a nation of missionaries. In addition to calling the nation as a whole to proclaim by word and lifestyle His truth to the world, God chose from within Israel special men to fulfill the missionary task. Those prophets first exhorted Israel to maintain her holy and righteous testimony; then they preached to the nations the message of repentance from sin, necessary because of God's coming judgment on the unbelieving world.

We have already seen how Abraham and Moses were prophetic voices to the peoples around them. The Old Testament major and minor prophets fulfilled a similar task as they preached to the pagan world: Isaiah (Babylon, Moab, Syria, Egypt, Tyre; chapters 13-27), Jeremiah (Egypt, Philistia, Phoenicia, Moab, Ammon, Edom, Syria, Kedar, Hazor, Elam, Babylon; chapters 46-51), Ezekiel (Tyre, Sidon, Egypt; chapters 25-32), Daniel (Babylon and Medo-Persia; throughout the entire book), Obadiah (Edom), Nahum (Nineveh), and Zephaniah (all unrepentant Gentiles).

Although most of us are familiar with the names of those prophets, many of us would find it difficult to recount their stories. However, there is one minor prophet (so-called because their writings are short, not minor in importance) with whom most believers, and even many unbelievers, have a great deal of familiarity. That prophet is Jonah. Although his example is primarily negative–an example by contrast–the Holy Spirit placed his story in Scripture because it is instructive for believers of all eras. He is the best biblical illustration of what a missionary should *not* be. The book of Jonah teaches us more about one man's poor attitude toward spiritual service and wrong methodology in ministry than does any other scriptural account of a person divinely called to a specific task.

We also learn from the book of Jonah how deeply concerned God is for the heathen and how utterly unconcerned proud Israel—personified in Jonah—was for them. That situation parallels the church today. Christians are as reluctant as Jonah to obey God's missionary call, and churches are as unconcerned about God's desire to reach the lost as Israel was.

Jonah's story illustrates what can occur when a believer is unwilling to exercise faith and respond obediently to God's call of service. It graphically describes a pattern of behavior that all genuine believers will strive to avoid if they would be Christians who walk by faith.

JONAH'S FIRST MISSIONARY CALL

God's first call to Jonah comes right at the outset of the book: "The word of the LORD came to Jonah the son of Amittai saying, 'Arise, go to Nineveh the great city, and cry against it, for their wickedness has come up before Me'" (1:1-2).

Relatively little is known of Jonah's background. He was the same prophet who predicted the restoration of the borders of Israel (the Northern Kingdom). That prophecy was fulfilled under Jeroboam II (2 Kings 14:25); the kingdom extended as far northeast as Damascus. Because Jonah spoke those words around 790 B.C., he likely knew Elisha and may have been taught by him (2 Kings 6:1-7).

During Jonah's time Israel prospered but also continued to endure guerrilla attacks from Syria and Assyria, whose capital was Nineveh. The Israelites thus came to fear Assyria's growing power and to hate the city of Nineveh and its people as enemies. The culturally-advanced city, located on the east bank of the Tigris River (and originally built by Nimrod; see Gen. 10:8-11), had a population of more than 600,000 at that time, and occupied an area that was huge. Archaeologists tell us it took three days to walk from one side of the city to the other.

The residents of Nineveh were proud of its grandeur, impressive size, and high level of civilization. But God was well aware of their wickedness and later, through the prophet Nahum, would speak against them again, denouncing them as a bloody people, full of fraud, lies, robbery, arrogance, sensuality, violence, witchcraft, and idolatry. The knowledge of man's wickedness ascends to the throne of God like acrid smoke from a fire (cf. Isa. 9:18; 65:5), and in His sovereign plan He first confronted Nineveh's sin by designating Jonah to bring the prophetic message.

God's First Commission to Jonah

When God commanded Jonah to "Arise, go to Nineveh the great city, and cry against it," He was sending him there not only to call Nineveh to repentance, but also to shame Israel in a dramatic way. Instead of proclaiming the one true God to the nations around them, the Jews had become entrenched in a proud, self-indulgent form of religion. Now their dreaded enemy, Assyria, was about to repent in sackcloth and ashes before Yahweh as a result of the simple preaching by an unknown prophet.

What a tremendous rebuke of Israel's attitude! Her own spiritual defection and unwillingness to obey God's will in evangelism caused the Lord to reprove her through Jonah. So God called an individual to do what His people were unwilling to do, and ultimately in the process He would both accomplish His mission to the Ninevites and severely admonish His own disobedient people.

Jonah's Disobedient Response

Incredibly, Jonah's response to God's first commission was a personification of Israel's unwillingness to reach out. The prophet reacted disobediently and "rose up to flee to Tarshish" (Jonah 1:3). Why would he respond in such a negative manner? There may have been some fear at the idea of entering the enemy's capital city and preaching to its residents. But Jonah 4:2 actually explains Jonah's most compelling motivation: "Therefore . . . I fled to Tarshish, for I knew that Thou art a gracious and compassionate God, slow to anger and abundant in lovingkindness, and one who relents concerning calamity." He could not tolerate the thought of God forgiving a Gentile nation that was an aggressor against and an oppressor of Israel.

The real issue for Jonah was not so much fear of going into an enemy city; rather, it was a deep ethnic and religious prejudice. He knew that if the Ninevites repented, God would forgive them, and he hated even the possibility of that happening. Feelings of racial prejudice ran deep in those days, just as they do with many people today. Jonah, like many of his Israelite contemporaries, despised the unsaved Ninevites and believed they deserved nothing but judgment and condemnation. He was afraid of the results if God's grace and mercy were applied to such a large group of Gentiles. He knew if they repented because of his preaching, they would be in a far better position before the Lord than the apostate Israelites. Jonah apprehensively envisioned the possible end of Israel's special election; if the Assyrians or any other Gentiles repented, God might bless them and withdraw His blessing from Israel.

Regardless of the reasons for Jonah's actions, his willful disobedience and its consequences ought to be a sober warning to all of us. He certainly knew he could not escape by ship from an omnipresent God. "Where can I go from Thy Spirit? Or where can I flee from Thy presence?" (Psalm 139:7). But he thought if he could get far enough away from Israel, he would no longer be available. If God really wanted someone to go to Nineveh, He would have to get someone else.

All believers probably have struggled to some extent with ministry availability. God has called all Christians to reach the people around them for Christ. But instead of accepting the call, many run the other way and get involved in their jobs, their activities, their families, and other obligations. I have known Christians who, when they sensed God's call to a special task, certain preparatory training, or a particular ministry (the pastorate, missionary service, Sunday school teacher), got themselves so entrenched in their present situation that they were unable to leave it and fulfill God's will.

Running from God's call, no matter what that might be, is like trying to run from light. You only end up in the dark. And that's literally what would happen to Jonah.

The Consequences of Jonah's Disobedience

Spiritual rebellion by a believer never ultimately succeeds. God always identifies the person and says, "You are the man!" (2 Sam. 12:7). Then that man or woman must face the consequences. That happened to Jonah when the Lord miraculously sent a powerful storm onto the Mediterranean Sea to intercept his ship as it headed for Tarshish, a commercial port in southwest Spain. The first chapter of Jonah describes the effects of the storm:

And the LORD hurled a great wind on the sea and there was a great storm on the sea so that the ship was about to break up. Then the sailors became afraid, and every man cried to his god, and they threw the cargo which was in the ship into the sea to lighten it for them. But Jonah had gone below into the hold of the ship, lain down, and fallen sound asleep. So the captain approached him and said, "How is it that you are sleeping? Get up, call on your god. Perhaps your god will be concerned about us so that we will not perish." And each man said to his mate, "Come, let us cast lots so we may learn on whose account this calamity has struck us." So they cast lots and the lot fell on Jonah. Then they said to him, "Tell us, now! On whose account has this calamity struck us? What is your occupation? And where do you come from? What is your country? From what people are you?" And he said to them, "I am a Hebrew, and I fear the LORD God of heaven who made the sea and the dry land." Then the men became extremely frightened and they said to him, "How could you do this?" For the men knew he was fleeing from the presence of the LORD, because he had told them. So they said to him, "What should we do to you that the sea may become calm for us?"-for the sea was becoming increasingly stormy. And he said to them, "Pick me up and throw me into the sea. Then the sea will become calm for you, for I know that on account of me this great storm has come upon you." However, the men rowed desperately to return to land but they could not, for the sea was becoming even stormier against them. Then they called on the LORD and said, "We earnestly pray, O LORD, do not let us perish on account of this man's life and do not put innocent blood on us; for Thou, O LORD, hast done as Thou hast pleased." So they picked up Jonah, threw him into the sea, and the sea stopped its raging. Then the men feared the LORD greatly, and they offered a sacrifice to the LORD and made vows.

—vv. 4-16

We can infer from this narrative that sin sometimes causes natural disasters that touch the lives of so-called innocent victims in ways they could never anticipate. The sailors on the ship with Jonah were suddenly forced to deal desperately with a hurricane-force storm that threatened their lives. Each in his own way sought divine intervention to rescue the ship from the emergency. But Jonah was not even on deck; he didn't want to think about God or talk to Him about anything. While the others struggled with the storm, he was down in the hold of the ship in a deep sleep of false security, trying to forget that God was after him.

Finally the pagan captain roused Jonah from sleep and urged him to pray to his God. Sadly, Jonah in his disobedience had been forced to acknowledge to the sailors that his God was the creator of the world (1:9). They had to exhort him to pray. Though a prophet, Jonah was useless to others, as are believers who fail to represent God well and bless people, or pull others into the consequences of their sinful problems.

When God revealed clearly to the sailors that Jonah was the offender who had brought on the storm, Jonah should have bowed in repentance and told God he would henceforth obey Him. But he was so rebellious and prejudiced that he said in effect, "I would rather die than preach God's grace to the Ninevites and see them converted and blessed by God." In contrast, the sailors were merciful and did not immediately toss Jonah overboard. Only after they failed in a last-ditch effort to bring the ship under control did they grant the runaway prophet his wish and throw him into the turbulent sea.

God immediately used that dramatic gesture to minister to the seamen. The sudden, supernatural cessation of the hurricane confirmed in their minds that Jonah truly had disobeyed his God. The calming of the storm was an evangelistic object lesson: "Then the men feared the LORD greatly, and they offered a sacrifice to the LORD and made vows" (v. 16). God was so intent on using Jonah that He used him in spite of his resistance, which is sometimes the painful way He uses unwilling believers today.

Jonah's Deliverance

By all natural appearances, when Jonah was thrown overboard he was as good as dead. But God was not through with the prophet. He was not going to allow Jonah to drown and give him the "luxury" of escaping his divinely appointed mission responsibilities. Instead, He sovereignly and supernaturally orchestrated events yet again: "And the LORD appointed a great fish to swallow Jonah, and Jonah was in the stomach of the fish three days and three nights" (Jonah 1:17).

Jonah's time inside the fish was a horrifying and unimaginable trial, but as a result he repented of his disobedience and recognized several key facts about God. First, he recognized God's presence and authority (2:1-6). Like the Prodigal Son in Luke 15, he knew God was in all that had happened and that he needed to submit to His authority. Second, Jonah recognized God's forgiveness and power (2:7-9). He realized he had to lose sight of his problems and focus only on God. He had forsaken the truth of God's mercy and blessing but was reminded that only God's saving power could restore him. Jonah recognized that "salvation is from the LORD" (2:9), and God honored his faith by commanding the fish to vomit him out onto dry land (2:10).

JONAH'S SECOND MISSIONARY CALL

God was so loving, gracious, and merciful with Jonah that after his restoration, He still wanted to use him. The very same commission the Lord gave in Jonah 1:2 He issued again: "Arise, go to Nineveh the great city and proclaim to it the proclamation which I am going to tell you" (3:2). This time Jonah had learned his lesson; in fact, he was a living model of one who had repented. So he obeyed and went to Nineveh.

Jonah's words to the Ninevites are summarized in a simple, straightforward message of judgment: "Yet forty days and Nineveh will be overthrown" (3:4).

The Consequences of Jonah's Preaching

What occurred next in Nineveh is stated matter-of-factly in the text: "then the people of Nineveh believed in God" (3:5). Yet it was nothing less than miraculous. God poured out on the entire city the grace to repent and believe. It was the greatest revival recorded in the Old Testament and perhaps included more conversions than any single event in redemptive history. The whole population (600,000 or more adults plus 120,000 children—see 4:11) turned to God, a far greater response than the 3,000 who believed on the Day of Pentecost (Acts 2:37-41). It's remarkable to realize that the Lord can use a chastened vessel like Jonah, who had been so stubbornly disobedient, to be the human instrument in turning an entire population from sin to genuine saving faith.

Jonah's Reaction to the Consequences

Unbelievably, Jonah's reaction to the revival in Nineveh reveals he was still struggling with a sinful, prejudiced attitude toward the people to whom he had just preached:

> *But it greatly displeased Jonah, and he became angry. And he prayed to the LORD and said, "Please LORD, was not this what I said while I was still in my own country? Therefore, in order to*

forestall this I fled to Tarshish, for I knew that Thou art a gracious and compassionate God, slow to anger and abundant in lovingkindness, and one who relents concerning calamity. Therefore now, O LORD, please take my life from me, for death is better to me than life."

—Jonah 4:1-3

The prophet would rather be dead than live with the fact that many thousands of a pagan, enemy nation had been converted. The Lord's reply to him was again gracious (v. 4). However, Jonah's heart had such a profoundly built-in nationalistic zeal for Israel that seeing God bring repentance to a large group of Gentiles, while so many of His own people were apostate, was more than Jonah could bear.

So he decided to camp near Nineveh, on the east side of the city, for forty days to see if the revival was real. If after forty days the response of the Ninevites proved hypocritical, he reasoned, the Lord would destroy them (inferred in Jonah's warning in 3:4.) So Jonah constructed a small lean-to to protect himself from the heat and waited to see if God might punish Nineveh after all.

God's Final Lesson for Jonah

In the midst of Jonah's renewed dissatisfaction, God used additional miracles to teach him one more profound lesson. The Lord provided an instant plant or tree for shade, appointed a worm to attack and destroy the plant the following dawn, and sent a hot east wind (sirocco) to bear down on Jonah and humble him (4:6-8).

Jonah's faithless response, which by now was normal for him, was to wish a third time that he could die. But God still was not finished with him and once again responded with patience and grace:

Then God said to Jonah, "Do you have good reason to be angry about the plant?" And he said, "I have good reason to be angry, even to death." Then the LORD said, "You had compassion on the plant for which you did not work, and which you did not cause to grow, which came up overnight and perished overnight. And

*should I not have compassion on Nineveh, the great city in which
there are more than 120,000 persons who do not know the difference between their right and left hand, as well as many animals?"*
                                                    —*4:9-11*

God was essentially telling Jonah that he had his perspective all
wrong. The prophet was very concerned about a transitory plant that
he had not even labored to make grow, and yet he was contemptuous
toward a whole city of people created in God's image, who would
have experienced eternal death had they not repented.

The Lord brought Jonah through a long, often painful series of
events to arrive at one great lesson: *he must get his priorities right.* Jonah
had to be broken of his selfishness and removed from his prejudice,
willfulness, and undue concern for his own comforts, and instead put
God and His message of salvation first. That's the same lesson
Christians today, by faith, need to learn. If those of us in the church
are going to be concerned about something, let it not be how well
shaded we are, but how well the unsaved world is hearing the Gospel
from us.

7

Mary:

A FAITHFUL

WORSHIPER OF GOD

History, both secular and sacred, has tended to romanticize Mary, the earthly mother of the Lord Jesus. Artists often portray her with a halo around her head and a mystical expression on her face. Of course, the Roman Catholic Church for centuries has presented her as larger than life, the perfect Madonna, the sinless, lifelong virgin, and the co-redemptrix (redeemer) who was taken bodily to heaven (much like Christ's ascension), where she was crowned "Queen of Heaven" and was given important mediatorial and intercessory roles (parallel to Christ's).

Such a broadly superhuman picture of Mary is without scriptural foundation. In reality, she was a common young woman from a working-class family. She could hardly have been more plain and unassuming. But her faith was extraordinary, a superior model of earnest, childlike, worshipful faith that is glad to accept the Lord's words without questioning. What an example Mary's faith is for today's Christians at a time when the church has largely replaced scriptural worship with superficial, man-centered formulas that miss the right attitude, object, and reason for worship. Mary had all three of these key worship ingredients in place, as this brief look at her life will reveal.

The Bible provides little detail about Mary's background. Comparing Matthew 27:56, Mark 15:40, and John 19:25, some have concluded that she had a sister named Salome, who was the mother of Zebedee's sons, the disciples James and John. We know for sure that Mary was related to Elizabeth, mother of John the Baptist (Luke 1:36). Mary's father-in-law, according to the genealogy in Luke 3:23, was Eli. Otherwise, all we know was that she spent her early life in Nazareth as the daughter of a poor but hardworking family.

MARY'S LIFE FOREVER CHANGED

Mary was likely in her late teens or early twenties when she had her profound and life-changing experience with God. Luke's Gospel introduces Mary and describes what happened:

> *Now in the sixth month [of Elizabeth's pregnancy] the angel Gabriel was sent from God to a city in Galilee, called Nazareth, to a virgin engaged to a man whose name was Joseph, of the descendants of David; and the virgin's name was Mary. And coming in, he said to her, "Hail, favored one! The Lord is with you."*
> *But she was greatly troubled at this statement, and kept pondering what kind of salutation this might be. And the angel said to her, "Do not be afraid, Mary; for you have found favor with God. And behold, you will conceive in your womb, and bear a son, and you shall name Him Jesus. He will be great, and will be called the Son of the Most High; and the Lord God will give Him the throne of His Father David; and He will reign over the house of Jacob forever; and His kingdom will have no end." And Mary said to the angel, "How can this be, since I am a virgin?" And the angel answered and said to her, "The Holy Spirit will come upon you, and the power of the Most High will overshadow you; and for that reason the holy offspring shall be called the Son of God. And behold, even your relative Elizabeth has also conceived a son in her old age; and she who was called barren is now in her sixth month. For nothing will be impossible with God." And Mary said, "Behold, the bondslave of the Lord; be it done to me according to your word." And the angel departed from her.*
> —1:26-38

All the elements in that passage—the angel, the Holy Spirit, the prophetic utterance, the Son of God conceived in Mary's womb, and Elizabeth's remarkable pregnancy—indicate the extraordinary and supernatural work that was occurring. Furthermore, the text, based on the Greek usage (the term has no valid alternate translation), clearly states that Mary was a "virgin," and so chaste and pure sexually.

Mary's supernatural pregnancy started during the *kiddushin* (engagement period) between Joseph, a local carpenter, and herself. In that society the engagement was as legally binding as the marriage (which is different from the custom in Western cultures today). During the twelve-month *kiddushin*, the man and woman were even called husband and wife, though they lived in separate homes and had no sexual relations. The period was intended to prove the fidelity of the couple, and if at any time during the betrothal either party was found to be unchaste, the contract was broken and divorce for infidelity was granted.

That provides some context to Matthew 1:19, "And Joseph her husband, being a righteous man, and not wanting to disgrace her, desired to put her away secretly." The news of Mary's condition undoubtedly shook Joseph's soul greatly, because he knew that a premarital pregnancy was not at all in accord with her righteous character. But no matter how perplexed and troubled he was, at least he did not have Mary put to death, as prescribed in Deuteronomy 22:20-21. Yet he knew he still had to divorce her and that he had to choose one of two ways to do it. He could either subject her to the personal shame and ruin of a public adultery trial, by which Mary would be convicted in front of everyone in town; or he could quietly write a bill of divorce before two or three witnesses and allow her to move somewhere else to secretly bear and rear the child.

Because he loved Mary, Joseph decided on the second option rather than the more painful first one. But then God's Spirit, by means of another angel, intervened, revealed the true circumstances of Mary's pregnancy, and rendered any divorce action unnecessary (Matt. 1:20-21). Thus Mary, who probably anticipated one of the two actions by Joseph and therefore could have doubted the wisdom of

Gabriel's words, was vindicated for her initial response of submissive faith and surrender to God's plan—"Behold, the bondslave of the Lord; be it done to me according to your word" (Luke 1:38).

Mary could hardly have had a more godly response to the announcement of Jesus' birth. It demonstrates that she was a young woman of mature faith and a worshiper of the true God.

MARY'S RESPONSE OF WORSHIP: THE *MAGNIFICAT*

Mary's humble and obedient reaction in Luke 1:38 was just the beginning of her wonderful response to the angel's announcement. She was not only convinced that she would give birth to the Lord (a fact confirmed by her cousin Elizabeth, verses 40-45), but was also filled with praise that she would be redeemed by that same Lord (cf. vv. 31-33).

Mary then launched into what I like to call "the hymn of the Incarnation," traditionally known as the *Magnificat*. Without question, it is a hymn of unspeakable joy, the most magnificent psalm of worship in the New Testament, an equal to any inspired Old Testament psalm, and very reminiscent of what we saw in Hannah's hymn of praise for the birth of Samuel (1 Sam. 2:1-10). Luke 1:46-55 records Mary's uplifting words:

> *My soul exalts the Lord, and my spirit has rejoiced in God my Savior. For He has had regard for the humble state of His bond-slave; for behold, from this time on all generations will count me blessed. For the Mighty One has done great things for me; and holy is His name. And His mercy is upon generation after generation towards those who fear Him. He has done mighty deeds with His arm; He has scattered those who were proud in the thoughts of their heart. He has brought down rulers from their thrones, and has exalted those who were humble. He has filled the hungry with good things; and sent away the rich empty-handed. He has given help to Israel His servant, in remembrance of His mercy, as He spoke to our fathers, to Abraham and his offspring forever.*

Mary's hymn of praise is instructive to us because of the three essential components of worship it contains: the attitude of worship, the object of worship, and the reasons for worship.

Mary's Attitude of Worship

Mary illustrates first of all that the proper attitude of worship is *internal*. When she said in verses 46-47, "My soul exalts the Lord, and my spirit has rejoiced in God my Savior," the terms "soul" and "spirit" both refer to one's internal state. They speak of the mind, emotions, and will—all the moral impulses and feelings of the human heart. Her use of such words ought to remind us that our worship is much more than being overwhelmed by impressive cathedral architecture or stained-glass windows, hearing uplifting organ or piano music, listening to the choir's anthem or the pastor's sermon, carrying or reading our Bible, bowing our head in prayer, or even partaking in the Lord's Supper. True worship can occur when those things are present, but they are external and not synonymous with it. Real worship happens when every element of our inner person comes together to blend into a great crescendo of praise and is presented in thankful thought and word to the Lord.

Mary was not guilty of the hypocrisy that Isaiah warned about: "This people draw near with their words and honor Me with their lip service, but they remove their hearts far from Me, and their reverence for Me consists of tradition learned by rote" (Isa. 29:13). Instead, she exhibited spontaneous but genuine worship from a heart that was so utterly consumed with the reality and wonder of God's person that she couldn't help but joyfully express it with all her external faculties.

Mary also demonstrates that true worship is *intense*. Her exclamation "My soul exalts the Lord" (v. 46) signified that her intensity was all-consuming. The Greek word translated "exalts" (*megalunei*) means "to cause to swell or to grow" and is sometimes translated "magnify" (KJV). That excellent translation suggests how a small object, when viewed through a magnifying glass, immediately grows much larger. The prefix *mega* denotes something that was extended or made large or very loud and was extremely intense. When Mary praised the Lord, she magnified His name and loudly extended her voice as she lifted up, extolled, and glorified Him.

Mary's worship attitude was anything but shallow or superficial, and that fact is further emphasized by verse 47: "my spirit has rejoiced in God my Savior." She was not simply uttering a few nice thoughts about God in a mild and controlled way. Rather, Mary was spontaneously bursting forth with vigorous praise from a heart filled with joy. "Has rejoiced" in the original (*agalliasen*) is another term of great intensity that referred to an out-loud, grand, swelling kind of joy. (It's the same root word used in 1 Peter 1:8, "you greatly rejoice with joy inexpressible and full of glory.") Mary truly exemplified what Jesus would later teach about worship: "those who worship Him must worship in spirit and truth [sincerity, intensity]" (John 4:24).

It is also notable that Mary's heart attitude of intense worship was *habitual*. The verb "exalts" (v. 46) is in the present tense, denoting continuous action. For Mary, genuine worship was part of her daily lifestyle, an attitude right in line with the apostle Paul's ambition expressed in Philippians 1:20: "Christ shall even now, as always, be exalted in my body, whether by life or by death." Whatever the circumstances and events of our life, we should be committed to worshiping our Lord every single day.

Finally, Mary is an excellent example of the truth that only *true humility* can give expression to true worship. For many of us, pride stands in the way of worship because we are more focused on ourselves than on God. But in Mary's song of praise, she focused on God, not herself. And when she did look at herself, it was only to acknowledge her own nothingness: "He has had regard for the humble state of His bondslave" (Luke 1:48).

Mary recognized her state of humiliation, lowliness, and spiritual unworthiness. That does not mean she was an ungodly or unrighteous woman. She was simply displaying the truest form of spirituality, that which does not give credit for righteousness to oneself. If Mary was the most favored, blessed, and exalted of all women, then, in keeping with Luke 14:11, she must actually have been the most humble of women: "he who humbles himself shall be exalted."

The Object of Mary's Worship

The object of Mary's praise and worship is obvious: "My soul exalts the Lord, and my spirit has rejoiced in God my Savior. . . . For the Mighty One has done great things for me; and holy is His name" (Luke 1:46-47, 49).

Mary worshiped God because she knew He is the only true object for our worship. "You shall fear only the LORD your God; and you shall worship Him, and swear by His name" (Deut. 6:13; cf. 10:20; Matt. 4:10; Luke 4:8). But, just as important, Mary worshiped God because He was her Savior who promised to redeem her from sin. In fact, the kind of intense and joyful worship Mary was engaged in has always been associated with salvation, as Zacharias, Simeon, and Anna would later demonstrate:

> *Blessed be the Lord God of Israel, for He has visited us and accomplished redemption for His people, and has raised up a horn of salvation for us in the house of David His servant.*
>
> —*Luke 1:68-69*

> *For my [Simeon's] eyes have seen Thy salvation, which Thou hast prepared in the presence of all peoples.*
>
> —*Luke 2:30-31*

> *And at that very moment she [Anna] came up and began giving thanks to God, and continued to speak of Him to all those who were looking for the redemption of Jerusalem.*
>
> —*Luke 2:38*

Historically, Roman Catholic commentators have tried to get around Luke 1:47 by claiming that because Mary was sinless, she called God her Savior only in the sense that He rescued her from her lowly estate and exalted her to be the queen of heaven. But that's a twisted and wrong interpretation. In Matthew 1:21, the angel speaking to Joseph makes it clear what kind of salvation Mary was talking about: "And she will bear a Son; and you shall call His name Jesus, for it is He who will save His people from their sins."

Years later Jesus would tell a crowd of followers, "'Who are My mother and My brothers?' And looking about on those who were sitting around Him, He said, 'Behold, My mother and My brothers! For whoever does the will of God, he is My brother and sister and mother'" (Mark 3:33-35). Even though the crowd had told Him His earthly family was looking for Him, Jesus did not interrupt His activities and give them special attention. Instead, He pointed out that being saved and obeying God were the most important things in life. Thus Mary was no different from anyone else. She acknowledged her sinfulness and need of salvation. That's why she rejoiced so enthusiastically when she learned that the Son of God she would bear would redeem her from her sin, along with all who trusted in Him.

The Reasons for Mary's Worship

There are three basic motives for Mary praising and worshiping God so fervently, all directly related to the truth of His salvation. First, she recognized *what God was doing for her*: "He has had regard for the humble state of His bondslave; for behold, from this time on all generations will count me blessed. For the Mighty One has done great things for me; and holy is His name" (Luke 1:48-49). Mary was amazed that an absolutely holy God would do such great things for one as unholy and undeserving as her. She was in no way commenting on her own greatness, but only on *God's* greatness. (Considering the phrase "all generations will count me blessed," Mary was not saying everyone would venerate her for her own transcendence. Rather, she was saying that everyone would remember how much God had blessed her.)

Mary then continued in her praise to God because of *what He will do for others*: "And His mercy is upon generation after generation towards those who fear Him" (v. 50). She paraphrased Psalm 103:17 (cf. Gen. 17:7; Exod. 20:6; 34:6-7) to express the fact that she was not by any means the only person God would bless with His saving mercy. Everyone who comes to Him with sincere awe and reverence for His holiness will receive His kindness. "How blessed is the man who fears the LORD" (Ps. 112:1). Mary was simply describing genuine believers, in future generations, who would fear the Lord.

The third reason Mary worshiped God with all her heart was because of *what He has done in the past*: "He has done mighty deeds with His arm; He has scattered those who were proud in the thoughts of their heart. He has brought down rulers from their thrones, and has exalted those who were humble. He has filled the hungry with good things; and sent away the rich empty-handed. He has given help to Israel His servant, in remembrance of His mercy, as He spoke to our fathers, to Abraham and his offspring forever" (Luke 1:51-55).

In typical Jewish worship fashion, Mary was reciting God's past faithfulness to His people (see Exod. 15; Judg. 5; Ps. 68, 78, 104, 105, 114, 135, 136, 145; Hab. 3). And she was extremely thankful that God, in His sovereign wisdom, has continually reversed the world's social order. Worldly people throughout the centuries who have lived in pride, self-sufficiency, and materialism eventually have been debased. But all those who have been meek and poor in spirit (Matt. 5:3-5) and who have sought God in repentance and faith have been lifted up.

It's obvious that Mary viewed God's redeeming actions as the reason we as believers ought to worship Him. There will be many times when we can't understand what He is doing or anticipate what He will do. But we can always reflect on what God has done for us and others. Mary is a role model of one who has supreme confidence in the righteousness of God's present actions and trust in the wisdom of His future plans, all based on the faithful and consistent record of what He has done in the past.

Mary is an example to us in her total response to the great news that she would, by the power of the Holy Spirit, help bring the Son of God, the Messiah, into the world. Her words and actions display a singular faith in which there was ultimately no questioning, doubt, fear, or misgiving, but only a confident submission that what the angel told her was true and was part of God's gracious plan.

8

JOHN THE BAPTIST:

THE

GREATEST MAN

===

Many years ago a young person asked me, "What makes a person great?" I didn't know precisely how to answer him, which started me thinking about the question. Many people believe greatness is the result of being born into a famous, wealthy, or influential family. Others believe acquiring wealth is a mark of greatness. Then there are those who believe academic degrees, business expertise, athletic ability, artistic talent, or high political or military office are necessary to be considered great.

Based on that set of criteria, even Jesus Christ was not great. While He manifested great wisdom and power, He was born into a common family—His father was a simple carpenter. When He was an adult, Jesus did not own a business, a herd of cattle or sheep, a house, or even a tent. He said, "The foxes have holes, and the birds of the air have nests; but the Son of Man has nowhere to lay His head" (Matt. 8:20). He had little, if any, formal education. And He certainly didn't seek political office or manifest any artistic accomplishments. Jesus displayed very little of the marks that the world would consider great.

John the Baptist manifested even fewer of the world's marks of greatness. Like Jesus, he came from a simple, obscure family. His father, Zacharias, was one of many priests who took turns ministering in the temple. His mother, Elizabeth, was also from the priestly tribe of Levi and a descendant of Aaron (Luke 1:5). But many were descendants of Aaron, and they had no special social status. It is likely that when John reached his teen years he went to live in the wilderness of Judea, existing much like a hermit and giving up any social honor and economic status or comfort.

But John was destined for greatness. John's father and mother "were both righteous in the sight of God, walking blamelessly in all the commandments and requirements of the Lord." But they had no children, and Elizabeth was beyond normal childbearing years (Luke 1:6-7). One day as Zacharias was ministering in the temple, "an angel of the Lord appeared to him, standing to the right of the altar of incense" (Luke 1:11). The angel said, "Elizabeth will bear you a son, and you will give him the name John. And you will have joy and gladness, and many will rejoice at his birth. For he will be great in the sight of the Lord" (vv. 13-15). Thus God named John and set him apart for greatness even before he was conceived!

John would "be filled with the Holy Spirit, while yet in his mother's womb. And he [would] turn back many of the sons of Israel to the Lord their God" (Luke 1:15-16). But his most significant task would be to "go as a forerunner before Him [Jesus] in the spirit and power of Elijah . . . so as to make ready a people prepared for the Lord" (v. 17). John's own father, himself "filled with the Holy Spirit," declared that John "will be called the prophet of the Most High; for you [John] will go on before the Lord to prepare His ways" (vv. 67, 76). "And the child continued to grow, and to become strong in spirit, and he lived in the deserts until the day of his public appearance to Israel" (v. 80).

That was John. His conception was miraculous, he was filled with the Holy Spirit before he was born, he was great in the sight of God, and he was to be the herald of the Messiah, announcing and preparing the people for His coming. So it is entirely right for Jesus to say of him, "Truly, I say to you, among those born of women there has not arisen anyone greater than John the Baptist" (Matt. 11:11). To emphasize the truthfulness of His statement, Jesus prefaced His words with "truly"—a term of strong affirmation often transliterated "Amen."

"Born of women" was a common ancient expression that referred to one's humanness (see Job 14:1; 15:14). Thus Jesus was saying that as far as mankind is concerned, no one who had yet lived was greater than John the Baptist. That means John was greater than Noah, Abraham, Isaac, Jacob, or Joseph. He was greater than Moses, Elijah, David, or any of the Old Testament prophets. He also was greater than any of the world's kings, emperors, philosophers, or military leaders. Thus John was the greatest man yet born besides Jesus Himself.

Jesus made sure, however, that the people did not misunderstand the nature of John's greatness: "Yet he who is least in the kingdom of heaven is greater than he" (Matt. 11:11). Although he was a spiritual giant, John's greatness came from his role in human history. In his spiritual inheritance John was equal to every other believer. That's why Jesus could say that the least in the kingdom of heaven (exaltation in the spiritual realm) "is greater than he" (exalted roles in the human realm), which included John.

What was it about John that led Jesus to speak of him in such glowing terms? In Matthew 11:7-14 Jesus sets forth three specific marks that characterize John's greatness.

JOHN'S PERSONAL CHARACTER

We have looked at several criteria the world uses to measure greatness. But I doubt anyone would argue the necessity of the need for strong personal character. John exhibits three vital character qualities.

Overcoming Weakness

Many people have difficulty rising above their difficulties and circumstances. Everyone has problems; overcoming them is what separates great people from indifferent people. Great people don't succumb to obstacles—they fight through them triumphantly. That's certainly what John the Baptist did when faced with doubts about Jesus' identity as the Messiah: "When John in prison heard of the works of Christ, he sent word by his disciples, and said to Him, 'Are you the Coming One, or shall we look for someone else?'" (Matt. 11:2-3).

John was filled with the Holy Spirit from his mother's womb and had been set apart by God to announce the Messiah and to prepare Israel for His coming. He had seen the Holy Spirit descend on Jesus at His baptism and had heard God the Father declare Jesus to be His beloved Son. From many sources, including some of his own disciples, he had heard of Jesus' miraculous powers. Yet John's lingering doubts troubled him because he likely felt they were a betrayal of the One he was sent to proclaim. Since he couldn't eliminate those doubts, he acknowledged them to his disciples and asked two of them to seek out Jesus and confirm the truth.

John only wanted to know the truth about Jesus; he was not jealously concerned about protecting his own ministry and his popularity among the multitudes. Fortunately his humility and underlying faith did not allow his doubts to grow into skepticism and denial.

John also showed no resentment of Jesus' popularity when it began to surpass his own. He even expected it: "He must increase, but I must decrease" (John 3:30). He confessed publicly that he was unworthy to remove Jesus' sandals; and when Jesus asked to be baptized by John, he replied, "I have need to be baptized by You, and do You come to me?" (Matt. 3:14).

Pride curses true greatness, and the person who, unlike John the Baptist, refuses to confess and overcome personal weaknesses is doomed to envy, hypocrisy, and mediocrity.

Holding Strong Convictions

A second aspect of John's personal character was his strong conviction. Since many who loyally followed John recognized him as "a prophet" with a divine message (Matt. 14:5; 21:26), they must have been confused by his doubts. Were he and his message no longer trustworthy?

To dispel their confusion, Jesus asked them a question: "What did you go out into the wilderness to look at? A reed shaken by the wind?" (Matt. 11:7). He appealed to their own experiences, asking them if John's preaching was ever uncertain and vacillating. Did he ever change his message or compromise his standards?

The reed Jesus referred to was native to Near Eastern riverbanks, including those of the Jordan where John baptized. Since the reeds were light and flexible, they would bend with every breeze. But the people knew that John didn't bend his resolve with every opposing wind. He stood up to the scribes, the Pharisees, the Sadducees, and even to Herod himself, which landed him in prison.

John had numerous opportunities to win the approval of the authorities. He was such a powerful and commanding figure that many thought he might himself be the Messiah (Luke 3:15). By compromising his convictions, John could have won the support of the hypocritical Pharisees and Sadducees who came to him for baptism. Instead, he confronted their sin and hypocrisy: "You brood of vipers, who warned you to flee from the wrath to come? Therefore bring forth fruit in keeping with your repentance; and do not suppose that you can say to yourselves, 'We have Abraham for our father'; for I say to you, that God is able from these stones to raise up children to Abraham. And the axe is already laid at the root of the trees; every tree therefore that does not bear good fruit is cut down and thrown into the fire" (Matt. 3:7-10). Speaking of Jesus, he continued, "And His winnowing fork is in His hand, and He will thoroughly clear His threshing floor; and He will gather His wheat into the barn, but He will burn up the chaff with unquenchable fire" (v. 12). Like William Penn, John believed that "right is right, even if everyone is against it, and wrong is wrong, even if everyone is for it."

Denying Self
Jesus challenged the crowd by asking them another question: "But what did you go out to see? A man dressed in soft clothing? Behold, those who wear soft clothing are in kings' palaces" (Matt. 11:8). His question reveals a third characteristic of John's greatness: his self-denial.

Great scientists often risk their health to make important discoveries. Great medical researchers risk exposure to deadly disease to save thousands of lives. Great artists and musicians sacrifice their social life to practice and perfect their craft. Great athletes constantly train their bodies, denying themselves pleasures most people take for granted. Great scholars study in isolation, sacrificing leisure and society. The easy way is never the way of success.

John's life could never be described as easy. He wore "a garment of camel's hair, and a leather belt about his waist; and his food was locusts and wild honey" (Matt. 3:4). John must have cut quite a startling figure. He was God's messenger, but he didn't live, dress, or talk like the other religious leaders of the day. John's garment of camel's hair and his leather belt were practical and durable, but certainly not comfortable or fashionable. In that sense he lived like the first Elijah (2 Kings 1:8). His diet of locusts and wild honey was as spartan as his clothing—nourishing perhaps, but little else.

John's very dress, food, and lifestyle were a stern rebuke to the self-satisfied and self-indulgent religious leaders of Israel—the scribes, Pharisees, Sadducees, and priests. Both physically and symbolically he separated himself from the hypocritical and corrupt religious and political systems. He was so consumed by God's calling that he was not attracted to the world's enticements. His devotion to ministry completely superseded any personal interests and comforts.

John's self-denial was also a rebuke to those who longed for their leaders' comforts although they couldn't indulge in their leaders' privileges. It was not John's plan, however, to turn the people into hermits or monks. His lifestyle was a dramatic reminder that worldly lusts and pleasures prevent people from following God's will completely and humbly.

As predicted before his birth, John had taken a lifelong Nazirite vow. The angel announced to Zacharias that John "will be great in the sight of the Lord, and he will drink no wine or liquor" (Luke 1:15). Along with abstaining from strong drink, the vow also involved never cutting one's hair or touching anything that was ceremonially unclean. Many Jews, both men and women, would take a Nazirite vow for a few months or years (Num. 6:4-8). But only Samson (Judg. 13:7; 16:17), Samuel (1 Sam. 1:11), and John the Baptist took the vow for life. John's lifelong, voluntary self-denial was the ultimate act of devotion to God.

JOHN'S PRIVILEGED CALLING

John's second mark of greatness was his privileged calling. Until Christ's ministry began, no one had ever been called to a task as lofty and sacred as that of John the Baptist.

In Matthew 11:9 Jesus asked the crowd a third question: "But why did you go out? To see a prophet? Yes, I tell you." The prophetic office began with Moses and extended until the Babylonian captivity. But 400 years passed before another prophet appeared in Israel, and that was John. You could call him the valedictorian of the Old Testament prophets. He was the most dynamic, articulate, confrontational, and powerful spokesman God had ever called. As the last of the prophets, his calling was to both announce the coming of the Messiah and to declare His arrival.

Jesus then assured the people that John was not just a prophet, but "one who is more than a prophet" (v. 9). Quoting Malachi 3:1, Jesus said, "This is the one about whom it is written, 'Behold, I send My messenger before Your face, who will prepare Your way before You'" (v. 10). The expression "before Your face" means "to be in front of" or "to precede." That means God sent John as His messenger to be the forerunner of the Messiah and to prepare the people for His coming. After thousands of years of God's preparation and prediction, John was given the unequaled privilege of being the Messiah's personal herald.

The Message

Part of preparing the people for the coming of the Messiah involved John's proclamation of a simple message, which is easily summarized in one word: "repent" (Matt. 3:2; cf. Acts 13:24; 19:4). The Greek word for "repent" means more than regret or sorrow (cf. Heb. 12:17);

it means "to turn around," "to change direction," "to change the mind and will." It doesn't refer to just any change, but always a change from wrong to right, from sin to righteousness. Repentance involves sorrow for sin, but sorrow that leads to a change of the will and conduct. Paul said, "The sorrow that is according to the will of God produces a repentance without regret, leading to salvation" (2 Cor. 7:10). John's command to repent could be rendered, "be converted." So his message of preparation for the coming of the King was repentance, conversion, and a demand for a completely different life.

That was a stark rebuke to the Jews who believed that as God's chosen people they deserved and were unconditionally assured of being in God's kingdom. John said, "Do not suppose that you can say to yourselves, 'We have Abraham for our father'; for I say to you, that God is able from these stones [Gentiles] to raise up children to Abraham" (Matt. 3:9). John's point was simple: "You are in the same condition as the Gentiles. [The Jews considered them to be dead and lifeless, much like stones.] You have no right to the kingdom unless you repent and are converted from sin to righteousness." Failure to repent and change one's sinful life would result in severe judgment. And when Jesus arrived on the scene, He also preached a message of repentance (Mark 1:15; cf. Matt. 4:17; Luke 5:32).

The Motive

The motive John gave for repentance was "the kingdom of heaven is at hand" (Matt. 3:2). The people needed to repent and be converted because the King was coming, and He deserves and requires no less. Only the repentant and converted can give the heavenly King the glory He deserves and enter His heavenly kingdom.

The Mission

The mission of John the Baptist had long before been described by Isaiah the prophet: "For this is the one referred to by Isaiah the prophet, saying, 'The voice of one crying in the wilderness, "Make ready the way of the Lord, make His paths straight!"'" (Matt. 3:3; cf.

Isa. 40:3-4). The greatest man who had yet lived was great primarily because he was the herald of the Messiah.

In ancient times a herald commonly preceded the arrival of a monarch, both to announce his coming and to prepare his travel arrangements. A coterie of servants would clear the road of rocks and debris, fill holes, and remove unsightly litter. As they cleared the way, the herald would proclaim the king's coming to everyone he encountered. His twofold duty was to proclaim and to prepare, and that is what John's ministry did for God's great King, Jesus Christ.

But as herald of the great King, John did not clear literal roads and highways of obstacles; he instead sought to clear men's hearts of the obstacles that kept them from truly worshiping and serving the King. The roadway of the Lord is the way of repentance, of turning from sin to righteousness and straightening crooked moral and spiritual paths. "Let every valley be lifted up, and every mountain and hill be made low," Isaiah continues, "and let the rough ground become a plain, and the rugged terrain a broad valley; then the glory of the LORD will be revealed, and all flesh will see it together" (Isa. 40:4-5).

John's crying in the wilderness of Judea was the urgent shouting of commanding people to repent, to confess sin and the need of a Savior. John called them away from the corrupt and dead religious system of their day—away from ritualism, worldliness, hypocrisy, and superficiality. John called them away from the cities and into the wilderness, to a place where people wouldn't go unless they were serious about repenting. In the wilderness they could listen, think, and ponder without being distracted by the religious leaders. In that desolate place they could begin to see the earthly greatness of John and the surpassing divine greatness of the One whose coming he announced.

The Ministry

The immediate effect of John's preaching was dramatic: "Then Jerusalem was going out to him, and all Judea, and all the district around the Jordan; and they were being baptized by him in the Jordan River, as they confessed their sins" (Matt. 3:5-6).

It is significant that those Jews submitted to John's baptism since it was completely different from the Levitical ceremonial washings, which consisted of repeated washings of the hands, feet, and head. Such washings represented repeated purification for repeated sinning.

John's baptism, however, was onetime. The only single washing the Jews performed was for Gentiles proselytes, and it symbolized their entrance into Judaism. So a Jew who submitted to John's baptism was demonstrating that he was actually like a Gentile, an outsider seeking entrance into the kingdom of God. Once-proud members of God's chosen race, descendants of Abraham and heirs of the covenant of Moses, came to John to be baptized like pagan converts to Judaism!

Unfortunately, subsequent accounts in the Gospels indicate that many of those acts of repentance were superficial and hypocritical, because John soon lost much of his following. But the impact of John's ministry on the Jewish people was profound and unforgettable (cf. Acts 19:1-7).

JOHN'S POWERFUL CULMINATION

A man with outstanding character and an outstanding calling must also have the opportunity to reach the potential of his greatness. God provided John the Baptist with that opportunity by planning his entrance into history at precisely the right time. After 400 years without a prophet in Israel, before Jesus began His ministry, John was the focal point of redemptive history and the culmination of Old Testament history and prophecy.

But John provoked conflict because his message upset the status quo. By calling for repentance, he stirred up the religious leaders and King Herod. And their response was often violent, eventually leading to his arrest, imprisonment, and execution. Jesus attested to that vicious response when he told the crowd: "From the days of John the Baptist until now the kingdom of heaven suffers violence, and violent men take it by force" (Matt. 11:12). Wherever he went, John evoked strong reaction.

The form of the Greek verb translated "suffers violence" can be read as either a Greek passive or middle voice. The middle voice fits the context best and refers to applying force or entering forcibly. So the verse could be translated, "The kingdom of heaven is vigorously pressing itself forward, and people are forcefully entering it." With its focus in John the Baptist, the kingdom moved relentlessly through the godless system that opposed it. Following the Lord necessarily requires sincere and tireless effort.

All of God's previous revelation culminated in John the Baptist. Jesus said, "For all the prophets and the Law prophesied until John. And if you care to accept it, he himself is Elijah, who was to come" (vv. 13-14). Through the last words of the last Old Testament prophet, God had said, "Behold, I am going to send you Elijah the prophet before the coming of the great and terrible day of the LORD. And he will restore the hearts of the fathers to their children, and the hearts of the children to their fathers, lest I come and smite the land with a curse" (Mal. 4:5-6).

Yet John said he was not the literal, resurrected Elijah most Jews expected (John 1:21), or that many Jews today expect. But he was the Elijah that the prophet Malachi predicted would come, as the angel confirmed to Zacharias: "It is he who will go as a forerunner before Him in the spirit and power of Elijah" (Luke 1:17). John was like Elijah—internally in "spirit and power" and externally in rugged independence and nonconformity.

Jesus' point in Matthew 11:14 was that if the Jews had believed John's message was from God and that Jesus was the Messiah, John would be the fulfillment of the Elijah predicted by Malachi. But if they refused to believe John's message, another Elijah-like prophet would come one day in the future. Because the Jews rejected John the Baptist as the true Elijah who was to come, they prevented the complete fulfillment of the prophecy as God had originally given it through Malachi. Another prophet like Elijah is yet to come before the Lord Jesus returns.

After John had been imprisoned and killed, Jesus confirmed the Jews' error: "'Elijah is coming and will restore all things; but I say to you, that Elijah already came, and they did not recognize him, but did to him whatever they wished.' . . . Then the disciples understood that He had spoken to them about John the Baptist" (Matt. 17:11-13).

THE PATTERN OF GREATNESS

Six things demonstrate the true greatness of John.

He was *filled with and controlled by the Spirit*, even from "his mother's womb" (Luke 1:15b).

He was *obedient to God's Word*.

He was *self-controlled*, drinking no "wine or liquor" (Luke 1:15a). He was temperate in his food, dress, and lifestyle.

He was *humble*. He had the right perspective in relation to Christ: "After me One is coming who is mightier than I, and I am not fit to stoop down and untie the thong of His sandals" (Mark 1:7), and, "He must increase, but I must decrease" (John 3:30).

He *courageously and faithfully proclaimed God's Word*.

Finally, he was *faithful in leading people to Christ*, in turning "back many of the sons of Israel to the Lord their God" (Luke 1:16).

John stands as a pattern for all who seek genuine greatness. Yet his greatness on earth was not equal to the greatness of all those who enter Christ's spiritual kingdom through trust in Him as Lord and Savior. True greatness ultimately means following in the footsteps of Christ, for He is the "one pearl of great value" worth sacrificing everything for (Matt. 13:46).

9

PETER:

LESSONS LEARNED

BY FAITH

Most believers can easily identify with the apostle Peter because his humanity comes through so often in the biblical record. (The only person mentioned more frequently in the four Gospels than Peter is Jesus Himself.) Our Lord spoke to Peter more often than to any of the other disciples, and in those encounters we often see that disciple's strengths and weaknesses on display. No other disciple so boldly, outspokenly, and repeatedly confessed and encouraged Christ as Peter did. Yet no other disciple so consistently interfered with, reproved, and confronted and tried to restrain Jesus as much as Peter did. Therefore the Lord had to speak both greater words of praise and blessing *and* sterner, more direct words of reproof to Peter than to any other of the twelve (except for His condemnation of the reprobate Judas Iscariot).

But the Lord used all of those blessings, corrections, and experiences to build Peter's faith and mold him into a godly leader. It was vital that Jesus shape his life if he was ever going to fulfill his calling as the influential leader of the early church (see Acts 1-12; 1 and 2 Peter).

In terms of function and rank, Peter was the foremost member of the disciples. This is indicated by the use of the Greek *pro-tos* (first in rank) in Matthew 10:2—"the first, Simon, who is called

Peter"—and even by the fact that all four New Testament lists of the apostles (Matt. 10:2-4; Mark 3:16-19; Luke 6:14-16; Acts 1:13) place Peter's name first. The twelve disciples were equal in their divine commission, authority, and power and will (except for Judas, replaced by Matthias) someday sit on equal thrones to judge the twelve tribes of Israel (Matt. 19:28). However, no group can operate properly without leadership, and Peter helped provide that for the twelve from the beginning.

Even the apostle's names provide insight into his character. His parents named him Simon, but Jesus changed that to Peter (*Cephas* in Aramaic), which means "stone" (Matt. 16:18). Peter was naturally vacillating and impulsive, and the other disciples likely wondered about the appropriateness of his new name. But the name change was perhaps an encouragement to Simon concerning the kind of solid man of faith Jesus wanted him to be.

For simple identification purposes, the Gospels refer to Peter as Simon (e.g., Mark 1:29-30; Luke 5:3, 10). Also, the Lord used his old name when reprimanding him for sin or notable displays of weakness, as when he doubted Jesus' directive to go "out into the deep water and let down your nets for a catch" (Luke 5:4). Jesus admonished him for lack of vigilance in the Garden of Gethsemane too: "Simon, are you asleep? Could you not keep watch for one hour?" (Mark 14:37). And Christ used Peter's former name after the Resurrection when He confronted him three times about his faithlessness (John 21:15-17). It appears that Jesus used "Simon" in those instances to remind Peter that he was behaving like his old self.

Peter was a native of Bethsaida but eventually moved to Capernaum. There he, his father John (Jonas), and his brother Andrew carried on their fishing business. How did Jesus take such a rugged tradesman, who was so inconsistent and self-centered, and transform him into a faithful leader of the apostles? The Gospels answer that question by revealing three elements that were foundational in forming Peter's character and nurturing his faith.

THE RIGHT POTENTIAL

Peter had good character and leadership potential, even though it was not always easy to discern. This was first evident in his tendency to *ask a lot of questions.* Many of those questions were superficial and immature, but nevertheless they showed a true concern for the Lord and His ministry. One who does not ask many questions will not likely become a successful leader, because he demonstrates little desire to learn or to be equipped to lead should the opportunity arise.

Peter seemed always eager to ask Jesus doctrinal and ministry-related questions. When he didn't understand the short parable about ceremonial uncleanness, he asked for an explanation (Matt. 15:15). When concerned about the rewards for discipleship, Peter did not hesitate to ask about them (Matt. 19:27). And along with James, John, and Andrew, he sought to know when and how the temple would be destroyed (Mark 13:4).

Jesus often answered Peter's questions in ways he did not expect, primarily because his queries usually missed the point of Jesus' teaching or were self-centered. Immature and misguided as many of his questions were, they allowed the Lord to work on building his faith.

Peter also manifested *initiative,* which is another characteristic of good leadership. He was often the first disciple to respond to Jesus' questions. It was Peter who declared, "Thou art the Christ, the Son of the living God" (Matt. 16:16) when Jesus tested the disciples concerning His true identity. Peter was also quick to react to what he saw on the mountain of transfiguration: "'Rabbi, it is good for us to be here; and let us make three tabernacles, one for You, and one for Moses, and one for Elijah.' For he did not know what to answer; for they became terrified" (Mark 9:5-6). Although his actions were often misguided (cf. John 18:10), Peter was always eager to support the Lord.

Finally, Peter usually was *at the center of activity.* He stayed close to Jesus and naturally wanted to be involved in every ministry event. Even when he denied Christ three times, he remained nearby, though his fellow disciples had all run away (Matt. 26:56-58, 69-75). When

Peter and John learned of Jesus' resurrection, John arrived at the tomb first only because he was a faster runner (John 20:4).

THE RIGHT EXPERIENCES

Our Lord also gave Peter all the necessary life experiences to help nurture his faith and develop his leadership potential. First, the apostle received certain *divine revelations*. At the momentous occasion when Peter first confessed Jesus as Christ, Jesus commented, "Blessed are you, Simon Barjona, because flesh and blood did not reveal this to you, but My Father who is in heaven" (Matt. 16:16-17). When many in the multitude stopped following Jesus because of His demanding teaching on discipleship, He asked the twelve, "You do not want to go away also, do you?" Peter again responded with understanding that could have come only from God: "Lord, to whom shall we go? You have the words of eternal life" (John 6:66-68).

God was establishing Peter's faith and transforming him into an instrument that would one day preach the Gospel. For instance, he was the Holy Spirit's spokesman on the Day of Pentecost: "Men of Judea, and all you who live in Jerusalem, let this be known to you, and give heed to my words" (Acts 2:14; cf. 4:8-12). And Peter would later record God's revealed truth in the two New Testament letters that bear his name.

Second, Peter experienced *great honor and reward from God*. Following the apostle's confession of Christ, Jesus told Peter, "I also say to you that you are Peter, and upon this rock I will build My church; and the gates of Hades shall not overpower it. I will give you the keys of the kingdom of heaven; and whatever you shall bind on earth shall have been bound in heaven, and whatever you shall loose on earth shall have been loosed in heaven" (Matt. 16:18). Peter's later ministry would unlock the doors of the Gospel to both Jews and Gentiles.

While Peter experienced great rewards and honors, he was also often the object of *great rebuke*. Sometimes his words contradicted the honors Jesus had previously bestowed on him. His statements could even reveal that his speech at times served Satan as well as God:

> *From that time Jesus Christ began to show His disciples that He must go to Jerusalem, and suffer many things from the elders and chief priests and scribes, and be killed, and be raised up on the third day. And Peter took Him aside and began to rebuke Him, saying, "God forbid it, Lord! This shall never happen to You." But He turned and said to Peter, "Get behind Me, Satan! You are a stumbling block to Me; for you are not setting your mind on God's interests, but man's.*
>
> —Matt. 16:21-23

When Peter elevated his own wisdom and understanding above the Lord's, he ceased serving God in faith and began serving Satan in the flesh.

God further permitted Peter the negative experience of *temporarily rejecting Jesus*. Just as extreme self-confidence resulted in Peter's rebuke by Jesus, it later resulted in his rejection of Jesus. Typical of Peter, he brashly denied the Lord's prediction that he and the other disciples would reject Jesus in the hours prior to His death: "Even though all may fall away because of You, I will never fall away" (Matt. 26:33). When Jesus stated more specifically that Peter would deny Him three times later that very night, Peter protested more strongly: "Even if I have to die with You, I will not deny You" (v. 35). But once again Jesus proved right and Peter wrong. As the apostle warmed himself in the high priest's courtyard, Peter not only denied Christ three times, but ever more vehemently each time (Matt. 26:69-75).

Peter's difficult experiences, however, did not ruin him or disqualify him from future ministry. Instead, he experienced a *recommissioning* from the Lord. When Jesus confronted Peter about his unfaithfulness and lack of love, Peter assured Him three times that he did indeed love Him:

*So when they had finished breakfast, Jesus said to Simon Peter,
"Simon, son of John, do you love Me more than these?" He said
to Him, "Yes, Lord; You know that I love You." He said to him,
"Tend My lambs." He said to him again a second time, "Simon,
son of John, do you love Me?" He said to Him, "Yes, Lord; You
know that I love You." He said to him, "Shepherd My sheep."
He said to him the third time, "Simon, son of John, do you love
Me?" Peter was grieved because He said to him the third time,
"Do you love Me?" And he said to Him, "Lord, You know all
things; You know that I love You." Jesus said to him, "Tend My
sheep. Truly, truly, I say to you, when you were younger, you used
to gird yourself, and walk wherever you wished; but when you
grow old, you will stretch out your hands, and someone else will
gird you, and bring you where you do not wish to go." Now this
He said, signifying by what kind of death he would glorify God.
And when He had spoken this, He said to him, "Follow Me!"*
—*John 21:15-19*

The Lord did not give up on Peter. He reassured him that he was
still an apostle and commanded him to exercise faith and obedience,
as Peter had done in the past, and to follow Him.

THE RIGHT ATTITUDES

The third major element in Peter's faithful learning process was
establishing the right attitudes. He acquired six essential ones as Jesus
continued to teach him principles of godly leadership.

First of all, our Lord knew Peter needed to learn *submission to
higher authorities*. In one remarkable and memorable lesson, the apostle learned about submitting to Jesus and to human authorities:

*And when they had come to Capernaum, those who collected the
two-drachma tax came to Peter, and said, "Does your teacher not
pay the two-drachma tax?" He said, "Yes." And when he came
into the house, Jesus spoke to him first, saying, "What do you
think, Simon? From whom do the kings of the earth collect cus-
toms or poll-tax, from their sons or from strangers?" And upon his*

saying, *"From strangers,"* Jesus said to him, *"Consequently the sons are exempt. But, lest we give them offense, go to the sea, and throw in a hook, and take the first fish that comes up; and when you open its mouth, you will find a stater. Take that and give it to them for you and Me."*

—Matt. 17:24-27

Peter was later able to articulate to members of the early church the lesson from that experience: "Submit yourselves for the Lord's sake to every human institution, whether to a king as the one in authority, or to governors as sent by him for the punishment of evildoers and the praise of those who do right. For such is the will of God that by doing right you may silence the ignorance of foolish men. . . . Honor all men; love the brotherhood, fear God, honor the king" (1 Pet. 2:13-15, 17).

Also, Peter really needed to learn the attitude of *restraint.* This was illustrated best in the garden when the mob came to arrest Jesus. Against overwhelming odds (a Roman army cohort numbered 500 or more), Peter drew his sword and began to resist those who wanted to seize the Lord. But Jesus ordered him to put down the sword and believe that God's plan would unfold: "Simon Peter therefore having a sword, drew it, and struck the high priest's slave, and cut off his right ear; and the slave's name was Malchus. Jesus therefore said to Peter, 'Put the sword into the sheath; the cup which the Father has given Me, shall I not drink it?'" (John 18:10-11).

Another vital attitude Peter came to learn was *humility.* As we have seen, Peter boasted, "Even though all may fall away because of You, I will never fall away" (Matt. 26:33) and then hours later denied Christ three times. Peter proved he was a different person years later when he said, "God is opposed to the proud, but gives grace to the humble" (1 Pet. 5:5).

A fourth attitude Peter had to learn was *sacrifice.* At the conclusion of Jesus' threefold reinstatement of him in John 21, Peter expressed concern about the apostle John's own sacrificial role: "Peter therefore seeing him [John] said to Jesus, 'Lord, and what about this man?'

Jesus said to him, 'If I want him to remain until I come, what is that to you? You follow Me!'" (vv. 21-22).

The Lord never again had to command Peter to follow Him. Thereafter he obeyed, no matter what the sacrifice, even if it involved suffering. Peter later wrote, "To the degree that you share the sufferings of Christ, keep on rejoicing . . . let those also who suffer according to the will of God entrust their souls to a faithful Creator in doing what is right" (1 Pet. 4:13, 19).

First Peter 4:8 records another lesson Peter learned: "Above all, keep fervent in your love for one another, because love covers a multitude of sins" (1 Pet. 4:8). Jesus wanted Peter to have the attitude of *love*—He pressed him about it three times in John 21:15-17 because He knew that no matter how much any ministry appeals to others, if it does not derive from love it is worthless. "If I give all my possessions to feed the poor, and if I deliver my body to be burned, but do not have love, it profits me nothing" (1 Cor. 13:3).

Finally Peter, as the leading member of Jesus' twelve disciples, needed to adopt an attitude of *courage*. He needed, by faith, to learn from his attempt to emulate Jesus in walking on the stormy Sea of Galilee:

> *And in the fourth watch of the night He came to them, walking on the sea. And when the disciples saw Him walking on the sea, they were frightened, saying, "It is a ghost!" And they cried out for fear. But immediately Jesus spoke to them, saying, "Take courage, it is I; do not be afraid." And Peter answered Him and said, "Lord, if it is You, command me to come to You on the water." And He said, "Come!" And Peter got out of the boat, and walked on the water and came toward Jesus. But seeing the wind, he became afraid, and beginning to sink, he cried out, saying, "Lord, save me!" And immediately Jesus stretched out His hand and took hold of him, and said to him, "O you of little faith, why did you doubt?" And when they got into the boat, the wind stopped.*
> —*Matt. 14:25-32*

Peter was no longer that fearful, doubting disciple when he stood boldly and confidently before the ruling Jewish council and proclaimed, "Let it be known to all of you, and to all the people of Israel, that by the name of Jesus Christ the Nazarene, whom you crucified, whom God raised from the dead—by this name this man [the one Peter had healed in Solomon's portico] stands here before you in good health. He is the stone which was rejected by you, the builders, but which became the very corner stone" (Acts 4:10-11). Peter was then completely confident in the Lord Jesus rather than in himself and could, along with John, resist the council's order to stop evangelizing: "Whether it is right in the sight of God to give heed to you rather than to God, you be the judge; for we cannot stop speaking what we have seen and heard" (vv. 19-20). At the prayer meeting that followed, their faith was strengthened further as they and other believers asked for courage, and "the place where they had gathered together was shaken, and they were all filled with the Holy Spirit, and began to speak the word of God with boldness" (v. 31).

Although Peter often learned his lessons slowly, he had the faith and perseverance to learn them well. He took the initiative to find a replacement for Judas (Acts 1:15-22), was a courageous spokesman for the Gospel (2:14; 4:8), first enacted church discipline (on Ananias and Sapphira, 5:3-9), confronted Simon the magician (8:18-23), and healed Aeneas and raised Dorcas from the dead (9:34, 40). And Peter recorded what he learned about submission, humility, sacrifice, love, and courage in his epistles. There he also exhorts us to supplement our faith with godly attitudes and character, so that we will trust God in any situation, obey His will, and glorify His name:

> *He has granted to us His precious and magnificent promises, in order that by them you might become partakers of the divine nature, having escaped the corruption that is in the world by lust. Now for this very reason also, applying all diligence, in your faith supply moral excellence, and in your moral excellence, knowledge; and in your knowledge, self-control, and in your self-control, perseverance, and in your perseverance, godliness; and in*

your godliness, brotherly kindness, and in your brotherly kind-
ness, love. For if these qualities are yours and are increasing, they
render you neither useless nor unfruitful in the true knowledge of
our Lord Jesus Christ.

                —2 Pet. 1:4-8; cf. 3:18; 1 Pet. 1:3-9; 4:7-10

PAUL:

TRANSFORMED FOR FAITHFUL MINISTRY

Church history is filled with stories of the amazing conversions of hardened sinners, people who never would have turned to Christ apart from the strength of the Gospel's transforming power. I think of John Newton, the slave ship captain who was saved after reading the devotional classic *The Imitation of Christ* (by Thomas à Kempis) and experiencing a frightening storm at sea. Along with other hymns, he wrote the much-loved "Amazing Grace." He also became a pastor and evangelical leader in eighteenth-century England. And he wrote this epitaph for his tombstone: "John Newton, clerk, once an infidel and Libertine, a servant of slavers in Africa, was, by the rich mercy of our Lord and Saviour Jesus Christ, preserved, restored, pardoned, and appointed to preach the Faith he had long laboured to destroy" (cited in Kenneth W. Osbeck, *101 Hymn Stories* [Grand Rapids, Mich.: Kregel, 1982], 28).

However, no spiritual transformation is as remarkable or has changed church history as much as that of Paul the apostle. His conversion was so important that the New Testament records it in three different, rather lengthy passages (Acts 9:1-31; 22:1-16; 26:4-18).

Paul, whose original name was Saul, was born in the important Roman city of Tarsus, in the province of Cilicia, near the border of Asia Minor and Syria. His citizenship was Roman (Acts 22:28), but his ethnic and religious background was Jewish. He received excellent training in Jerusalem as a Pharisee, studying under Gamaliel, the most respected rabbi of that day.

Saul is first mentioned in Scripture in connection with the stoning of Stephen (Acts 7:58), which implies he had a leading role in that sinful action. He was definitely the leader of the vicious persecution of the church following Stephen's death (8:1-3). Saul later described his role in greater detail before Agrippa: "So then, I thought to myself that I had to do many things hostile to the name of Jesus of Nazareth. And this is just what I did in Jerusalem; not only did I lock up many of the saints in prisons, having received authority from the chief priests, but also when they were being put to death I cast my vote against them. And as I punished them often in all the synagogues, I tried to force them to blaspheme; and being furiously enraged at them, I kept pursuing them even to foreign cities" (26:9-11).

Saul indeed became obsessed with persecuting Christians. When he heard about a group of them in Damascus, the ancient capital of Syria, he "went to the high priest, and asked for letters from him to the synagogues at Damascus, so that if he found any belonging to the Way [Christians], both men and women, he might bring them bound to Jerusalem" (Acts 9:1-2). The dispute between Saul and his supporters and Christ's followers was still seen by the Romans as an internal Jewish matter. Therefore, as recognized head of the Jewish state, the high priest had to issue authority to Saul for the apprehension of Christians.

Saul obtained the necessary permission papers from the high priest and set out for Damascus with his companions. Little did he realize that before arriving in the city he would have an encounter with the risen and ascended Christ that would turn his world inside-out and upside-down.

PAUL COMES TO FAITH IN CHRIST

The first phase of Saul's salvation experience is that *he came into direct contact with Jesus Christ.* As he intently pressed on toward Damascus, his progress was abruptly stopped by a blinding light from heaven.

The light transcended the brilliance of the noonday sun (Acts 26:13) because it was a blazing, glorious appearance of the Lord Jesus Christ. Such an awesome sight caused Saul to fall to the ground in terror. He actually saw Jesus in all His glorious brilliance and understood the convicting words He spoke, whereas his companions saw only the light and heard nothing but noise (22:9).

Although God does not confront all men and women as dramatically as He did Saul, He always sovereignly begins the process of their coming to Christ (cf. John 6:37, 44; 10:27-29; 2 Cor. 4:6; Phil. 1:29). Saul, through this stunning encounter, understood that truth and later faithfully taught it to others:

> *For we also once were foolish ourselves, disobedient, deceived, enslaved to various lusts and pleasures, spending our life in malice and envy, hateful, hating one another. But when the kindness of God our Savior and His love for mankind appeared, He saved us, not on the basis of deeds which we have done in righteousness, but according to His mercy, by the washing of regeneration and renewing by the Holy Spirit.*
>
> *—Titus 3:3-5*

During Saul's face-to-face encounter with the Lord, *he immediately heard the words of divine conviction.* Christ's words, "Saul, Saul, why are you persecuting Me?" (Acts 9:4) were intended to bring anguish to his soul, to make him realize how wrong he had been, and to overwhelm him with guilt for hating Jesus without a cause (cf. John 15:25). The enormity of Saul's crimes was not merely that he had persecuted believers, but that he had persecuted their Head, the Lord Jesus.

The sin that ultimately condemns people to hell is a lasting refusal to love and obey Christ, and genuine salvation must include personal conviction of that sin. Through his own knowledge of the Christian faith and redemptive history, having witnessed directly or indirectly the words and works of the apostles, Saul had been prepared by the Holy Spirit for that moment on the Damascus road.

Whereas once he intellectually knew the claims of Jesus, then he was brought low and made willing to believe them from the heart.

In response to his divine humbling, *Saul had a definite and thorough conversion experience.* When he heard the Lord say, "I am Jesus whom you are persecuting" (Acts 9:5), he immediately realized that Jesus really was the risen Messiah, His Gospel was God's truth, and he, Paul, had been fighting against God. At that instant Saul's resistance collapsed, and he turned to the Lord in repentance and faith. In his letter to the Philippians he describes the profound change that occurred in his soul in those hours:

> *If anyone else has a mind to put confidence in the flesh, I far more: circumcised the eighth day, of the nation of Israel, of the tribe of Benjamin, a Hebrew of Hebrews; as to the Law, a Pharisee; as to zeal, a persecutor of the church; as to the righteousness which is in the Law, found blameless. But whatever things were gain to me, those things I have counted as loss for the sake of Christ. More than that, I count all things to be loss in view of the surpassing value of knowing Christ Jesus my Lord, for whom I have suffered the loss of all things, and count them but rubbish in order that I may gain Christ, and may be found in Him, not having a righteousness of my own derived from the Law, but that which is through faith in Christ, the righteousness which comes from God on the basis of faith, that I may know Him, and the power of His resurrection and the fellowship of His sufferings, being conformed to His death; in order that I may attain to the resurrection from the dead.*
>
> —3:4-11

Saul's miraculous conversion is truly a testimony to the extent and power of God's sovereign grace. After that day on the way to Damascus, the apostle gave just one explanation for what happened to him: God intervened so that he came face-to-face with the risen, glorified Christ and by faith embraced Him as his Lord and Savior (see 1 Tim. 1:13-16).

The genuineness of Saul's salvation was apparent right away

because *he was obedient to the lordship of Christ.* Immediately he submitted himself to the will of the Lord he had long despised and fought against: "And I said, 'What shall I do, Lord?' And the Lord said to me, 'Arise and go on into Damascus; and there you will be told of all that has been appointed for you to do.' But since I could not see because of the brightness of that light, I was led by the hand by those who were with me, and came into Damascus" (Acts 22:10-11). Thus Saul's entry into the city was not at all what he had anticipated. Rather than entering triumphantly and apprehending all the Christians as he had originally planned, he entered in humiliation and blindness as a Christian, seeking to know what God would have him do during the remainder of his life.

As part of his consecration to the Lord, God gave Saul some time to meditate on his astonishing transformation. Acts 9:9 says, "He was three days without sight, and neither ate nor drank." During that time God undoubtedly helped Saul reconstruct and reevaluate his entire life and purpose. The newly called apostle began the journey toward spiritual growth and sanctification that would last until he died.

PAUL BECOMES DEVOTED TO PRAYER

During his three days of meditation and reflection, Saul became a man of unceasing prayer. Like anyone who is truly changed by the grace of God, Saul found prayer to be the spontaneous response to his new faith in the Savior.

While Saul waited, fasted, and prayed, God gave him a vision that a man named Ananias would lay hands on him and restore his sight (Acts 9:12). Ananias is described as a man who was "devout" and "well spoken of by all the Jews who lived" in Damascus (22:12). He was one of the leaders of the Damascus church and therefore would have been one of Saul's primary targets for arrest. But in a separate vision, the Lord told Ananias about Saul's vision and told him to visit the man from Tarsus (9:10-11).

Although it would have been difficult for him (cf. Acts 9:13-14), not yet knowing of Saul's conversion, Ananias was willing to be an instrument God could use to fulfill Saul's hope of receiving his eyesight again.

PAUL EMBARKS ON A LIFE OF SERVICE

The amazing turn of events in Saul's life continued as God's visions to him and Ananias were fulfilled and the two men met. Ananias's doubts and hesitations about seeing Saul, due to the great persecutor's reputation among believers, were quickly set aside: "But the Lord said to him [Ananias], 'Go, for he [Saul] is a chosen instrument of Mine, to bear My name before the Gentiles and kings and the sons of Israel; for I will show him how much he must suffer for My name's sake'" (Acts 9:15-16).

The Lord's words in verses 15-16 prove again that the call to spiritual service is not based on human wisdom but on the sovereign will of God. Saul understood this truth early in his Christian pilgrimage, and it was demonstrated regularly throughout his ministry as the apostle Paul. "Paul, an apostle (not sent from men, nor through the agency of man, but through Jesus Christ, and God the Father, who raised Him from the dead)" (Gal. 1:1; cf. 1 Tim. 2:7; 2 Tim. 1:11). "I was made a minister according to the stewardship from God" (Col. 1:25).

Of course, the plans God revealed for Saul in Acts 9:15-16 were also carried out in the years to come. He often preached to the Jews first (Acts 13:14; 14:1; 17:1, 10; 18:4; 19:8), so that he could fulfill his primary calling to the Gentiles (Rom. 11:13; 15:16). He also took God's Word before kings, such as Agrippa (Acts 25:23ff.) and, very likely, Caesar (cf. 2 Tim. 4:16-17).

Before long God also began to fulfill the promise that Saul would have to suffer much and often for the sake of Christ. And in the years to come the apostle lived out the reality of that promise very well (1 Cor. 4:9-13; 2 Cor. 11:23-29; 12:7-10).

Saul began his long road of service and suffering when Ananias finally met him. Their encounter involved more than a laying on of hands to restore Saul's sight. It was also the time of Saul's formal commissioning to the ministry: "And [Ananias] said, 'The God of our fathers has appointed you to know His will, and to see the Righteous One, and to hear an utterance from His mouth. For you will be a witness for Him to all men of what you have seen and heard'" (Acts 22:14-15). Thereafter Saul would consistently advocate that he and all believers must be always serving the Lord, as he told the Corinthians: "Let a man regard us in this manner, as servants of Christ, and stewards of the mysteries of God" (1 Cor. 4:1).

PAUL IS FILLED WITH THE HOLY SPIRIT

An important part of Saul's commissioning was his filling by the Holy Spirit (Acts 9:17). Obviously the Spirit had already worked in his life to bring him to salvation. He had convicted Saul of sin (John 16:9), convinced him of the lordship of Christ (1 Cor. 12:3), converted him (John 3:5; Titus 3:5), and placed him into Christ's body, the church, and indwelt him permanently (1 Cor. 12:13). But now Saul needed to be filled with the Holy Spirit in a manner that specially empowered him for the Lord's service (cf. Acts 2:4, 14; 4:8, 31; 6:5, 8).

Saul received the Spirit at his commissioning without the assistance or approval of any of the other apostles and without the dramatic outpouring of the Spirit that occurred at Pentecost. Saul was an apostle in his own right, called personally by Jesus Christ, not by the other apostles (Gal. 1:1, 15-17; cf. 1 Cor. 9:1).

The first major way the Holy Spirit transformed Saul was to refine his natural strengths. Saul's strength of leadership gifts, willpower, motivation, convictions, knowledge, public speaking ability, and his wise use of time and talents were all channeled for the Lord's purposes.

The second way the Spirit molded Saul was to replace undesirable personal traits with desirable ones. The Spirit replaced his natural hatred with love, his aggressiveness with peacefulness, his harsh treatment of people with gentleness, and his pride with humility.

Saul later acknowledged gratefully that the Holy Spirit is at work sanctifying all Christians: "But we all, with unveiled face beholding as in a mirror the glory of the Lord, are being transformed into the same image from glory to glory, just as from the Lord, the Spirit" (2 Cor. 3:18).

PAUL ENJOYS FELLOWSHIP WITH BELIEVERS

Saul's first outward act of obedience following his commissioning was to obey Ananias's exhortation (Acts 22:16) and be baptized. That action openly identified Saul with the very people he had hated and persecuted.

He then enjoyed fellowship for several days with the believers in Damascus (Acts 9:18-19). That no doubt gave them time to celebrate Saul's conversion and minister to his needs.

Such a desire for Christian fellowship is another sure mark of a divinely changed life. The apostle John reminds us, "We know that we have passed out of death into life, because we love the brethren. He who does not love abides in death" (1 John 3:14). Genuine believers will also agree, as Saul would have, with the psalmist's words: "I am a companion of all those who fear Thee, and of those who keep Thy precepts" (Ps. 119:63).

PAUL FIRST PREACHES JESUS

With his life now irrevocably transformed, Saul wasted no time in launching his ministry of preaching and teaching the Gospel of Jesus Christ:

> And immediately he began to proclaim Jesus in the synagogues, saying, "He is the Son of God." And all those hearing him continued to be amazed, and were saying, "Is this not he who in Jerusalem destroyed those who called on this name, and who had come here for the purpose of bringing them bound before the chief priests?" But Saul kept increasing in strength and confounding the Jews who lived at Damascus by proving that this Jesus is the Christ.
>
> —*Acts 9:20-22*

If the Christians in Damascus were shocked and pleasantly surprised by Saul's conversion, the Jews were shocked and incensed at his preaching. They had expected him to take Christians prisoner, not proclaim Jesus as Lord in the synagogues. But from the outset of his ministry, Saul felt a courageous drive: "Woe is me if I do not preach the gospel" (1 Cor. 9:16).

The upheaval that Saul's preaching caused among the Jews is difficult for us to identify with. But it should not be surprising that they would not have understood the drastic change in Saul's allegiance. After all, the most zealous defender of Judaism had now become the most ardent evangelist for Christianity.

But Saul did not retreat one step in the face of all the Jewish hostility. Instead, he "kept increasing in strength and confounding the Jews who lived at Damascus by proving that this Jesus is the Christ" (Acts 9:22). That he should succeed in debating the unbelieving Jews, as Stephen had done before him, should not surprise any student of Scripture. Now that Saul knew who Jesus really was, he could combine that knowledge with his excellent Jewish education and extensive understanding of the Old Testament to prove that Jesus was the long-awaited Messiah.

PAUL FIRST ENCOUNTERS PERSECUTION

Saul's initial efforts at ministry led to his taking some extended time (probably three years) away from the centers of activity in Jerusalem and Damascus: "I did not immediately consult with flesh and blood, nor did I go up to Jerusalem to those who were apostles before me; but I went away to Arabia, and returned once more to Damascus. Then three years later I went up to Jerusalem to become acquainted with Cephas, and stayed with him fifteen days" (Gal. 1:16-18). Paul's words imply that as the newly converted Saul of Tarsus he had learned directly from the Lord in Nabatean Arabia.

When Saul returned to Damascus, he preached the Gospel more powerfully than before, which turned the Jews entirely against him and necessitated his escape from their deadly persecution: "The Jews plotted together to do away with him, but their plot became known to Saul. And they were also watching the gates day and night so that they might put him to death; but his disciples took him by night, and let him down through the opening in the wall, lowering him in a basket. And when he had come to Jerusalem, he was trying to associate with the disciples; and they were all afraid of him, not believing that he was a disciple" (Acts 9:23-26).

When Saul arrived in Jerusalem and tried to affiliate with the other apostles, he must have seemed like an impostor. What if he was trying to destroy from within what he could not destroy from without? The Greek verb for "was trying" is in the imperfect tense, suggesting that repeated attempts by Saul to break the impasse with the other disciples were rebuffed (Act 9:26). It was not until the highly regarded Barnabas (cf. 4:36) vouched for Saul that he was finally accepted by the church in Jerusalem (9:27).

The believers, however, soon found it was nearly as bad having Saul on their side as against them. His bold preaching stirred up further opposition from the Hellenistic Jews, and there were new efforts to kill him. When the church learned of the latest plot, the members made sure Saul could escape again, this time to Caesarea (a seaport on the Mediterranean) and on back to his hometown of Tarsus (Acts 9:29-30; cf. 22:17-21).

Saul then was off the center stage for a few years, but he was far from inactive. He was undoubtedly vigorously obeying God's call and planting churches in various locations (cf. Acts 15:23; Gal. 1:21). That was the beginning of his period of influence on the New Testament church, during which Saul (soon to be Paul) recorded and implemented divine principles of ministry. Those principles are still God's standard for churches and believers today, as Paul's words in his letters and even in Acts so clearly indicate.

PAUL'S VIEW OF MINISTRY

If Paul ministered today, he would be sought after and copied more than any church growth expert. Leaders would figure there must be something to his methods since they resulted in the spread of Christianity throughout the Mediterranean world. But it would be wrong to seek to duplicate his "formula for success" because his attainments did not result from mere methodology. The apostle's successful ministry was based on devotion to God's truth, spiritual character, service to the Lord, and the example he set for his followers. Paul was thoroughly committed to the principle of leadership by example (cf. John 13:15; 1 Cor. 4:16; Phil. 3:17; Heb. 13:7; 1 Pet. 5:3).

Acts 20:17-24 contains perhaps the first detailed New Testament exposition of Paul's ministry perspective. His focus was on godly attitudes regarding four areas: God, the church, the lost, and himself. If these attitudes are right and according to God's will, the foundation will be established for any servant of Christ to have a successful ministry.

An Attitude of Service Toward God

The apostle Paul often referred to himself as a "bond-servant of Christ Jesus" (Rom. 1:1; cf. Gal. 1:10; Col. 1:7; 4:7; Titus 1:1). He wrote to the Thessalonians, "Just as we have been approved by God to be entrusted with the gospel, so we speak, not as pleasing men but God, who examines our hearts" (1 Thess. 2:4).

First of all, Paul knew that a servant of the Lord would serve Him in *humility*, because a servant is not greater than his master (Matt. 10:24). Paul exemplified humility throughout his ministry, and he acknowledged that truth to the Ephesian elders: "serving the Lord with all humility and with tears and with trials" (Acts 20:19). Paul also often expressed his humility in his epistles, perhaps best summarized in 2 Corinthians 3:5: "Not that we are adequate in ourselves to consider anything as coming from ourselves, but our adequacy is from God" (cf. 1 Cor. 3:5; 15:9; Eph. 3:8; 1 Tim. 1:15-16).

In addition to humility, Paul declared that any servant of God must be *willing to suffer for His sake*. We have already seen that the apostle experienced persecution early in his Christian life (Acts 9:23-24), but in Acts 20:19 he mentions two specific ways in which suffering comes to the true servant.

"With tears" refers to *internal suffering*, the grief and pain Paul felt whenever God was dishonored. Three realities in his ministry especially caused tears for the apostle. First was the condition of the lost. "I have great sorrow and unceasing grief in my heart. For I could wish that I myself were accursed, separated from Christ for the sake of my brethren [the Jews], my kinsmen according to the flesh" (Rom. 9:2-3).

Second, there was the struggle experienced by weak and sinning believers. He expressed his sincere concern for such brethren at Corinth: "Out of much affliction and anguish of heart I wrote to you with many tears" (2 Cor. 2:4).

Third, there was the threat posed by false teachers, which caused Paul to caution the Ephesian elders, "Therefore be on the alert, remembering that night and day for a period of three years I did not cease to admonish each one with tears" (Acts 20:31; cf. Phil. 3:18).

Paul also had to deal with much *external suffering*, most of it deriving, in his words, from the "trials which came upon me through the plots of the Jews" (Acts 20:19). In defending the integrity of his ministry to the Corinthians, he outlined the broad scope of opposition he endured:

> *Five times I received from the Jews thirty-nine lashes. Three times I was beaten with rods, once I was stoned, three times I was shipwrecked, a night and a day I have spent in the deep. I have been on frequent journeys, in dangers from rivers, dangers from robbers, dangers from my countrymen, dangers from the Gentiles, dangers in the city, dangers in the wilderness, dangers on the sea, dangers among false brethren; I have been in labor and hardship, through many sleepless nights, in hunger and thirst, often without food, in cold and exposure. Apart from such external things, there is the daily pressure upon me of concern for all the churches.*
> *—2 Cor. 11:24-28*

Paul truly demonstrated that the genuine measure of a minister for Christ is whether or not he focuses solely on pleasing God. Like

Paul, he will be willing to serve humbly and to endure persecution from those opposed to the truth.

An Attitude of Instruction Toward the Church

Paul knew his ministry to the church was primarily a teaching one (Eph. 4:12). That's why he reminded the Ephesian elders that he "did not shrink from declaring to you anything that was profitable, and teaching you publicly and from house to house" (Acts 20:20). In the Greek, "shrink from" means "to draw back" or "to withhold." Paul did neither of those when he taught, admonished, and exhorted the churches. He imparted all of God's wise counsel and anything of His holy, sovereign purpose that was profitable to the believers.

In his instructional ministry Paul played no favorites (cf. Gal. 1:10). He boldly confronted everyone as needed, even the apostle Peter when he was guilty of hypocrisy or Barnabas when he compromised scriptural truth (Gal. 2:11-21). When Paul commanded Timothy to "preach the word; be ready in season and out of season; reprove, rebuke, exhort, with great patience and instruction" (2 Tim. 4:2), the apostle was already an example of one who taught in those very ways.

Paul's teaching had both public and private outlets. Acts 19:8 says he taught in the synagogue at Ephesus for three months and then in a rented hall for two more years (19:9-10). Those publicly proclaimed truths of God were also sometimes taught privately and applied to the daily concerns of families and individuals "from house to house" (20:20).

In whatever context he taught, Paul, as a faithful servant of the Lord Jesus, always proclaimed the entire spectrum of truth from God's Word. And he did it in such a way that he was consistently a "workman who does not need to be ashamed, handling accurately the word of truth" (2 Tim. 2:15).

An Attitude of Evangelism Toward the Lost

The third aspect of Paul's ministry perspective is his burden for those who did not know Christ. He knew he had a mandate for evangelism:

"I am under obligation both to Greeks and to barbarians, both to the wise and to the foolish.... For I am not ashamed of the gospel, for it is the power of God for salvation to everyone who believes, to the Jew first and also to the Greek" (Rom. 1:14, 16; cf. 1 Cor. 9:19-23).

Paul's evangelism was always thorough, as indicated by what he told the Ephesian leaders: "solemnly testifying to both Jews and Greeks of repentance toward God and faith in our Lord Jesus Christ" (Acts 20:21). His Gospel presentations were always detailed and comprehensive, containing two crucial, divinely ordered components.

First, Paul always exhorted the unsaved to repent. The Greek term for *repentance* means "to change one's mind or purpose" and describes a change of mind that results in a change of behavior. In the conversion process, the sinner consciously turns intellectually, emotionally, and volitionally from his sins to God (see Acts 2:36-41).

Paul's evangelistic method simply followed Jesus' prescription that "repentance for forgiveness of sins should be proclaimed in His name to all the nations, beginning from Jerusalem" (Luke 24:47; cf. Acts 17:30). That sets forth repentance as central to the true Gospel message (cf. Matt. 4:17; Luke 3:8; 5:32; Acts 26:20).

Paul's evangelistic appeals also included a call to have "faith in our Lord Jesus Christ" (Acts 20:21; cf. 1 Thess. 1:9). And Paul knew that saving faith involved, like repentance, the whole person. One must intellectually know, emotionally assent to, and willingly trust in the substance of the Gospel message.

Paul was not only a servant who taught and built up the household of God, but he was a faithful herald, proclaiming the Gospel of Jesus Christ to lost sinners.

Paul's Sacrificial Attitude Regarding His Own Life

Paul's fourth attitude of servanthood, revealed in Acts 20, is the single-minded devotion he had to his calling as an apostle. Even though the Holy Spirit revealed to him that he faced some as-yet-undefined persecution in Jerusalem, the apostle's faithful sense of duty to Christ compelled him to continue: "Behold, bound in spirit, I am on my way to Jerusalem, not knowing what will happen to me there, except that the Holy Spirit solemnly testifies to me in every city, saying that bonds and afflictions await me" (Acts 20:22-23; cf. Rom. 15:31).

Paul's response to his difficult situation demonstrates his genuine sacrificial attitude in ministry. The only thing that mattered to him was to fulfill his apostolic mission: "I do not consider my life of any account as dear to myself, in order that I may finish my course, and the ministry which I received from the Lord Jesus, to testify solemnly of the gospel of the grace of God" (Acts 20:24). When compared to God's work, what happened to his life was not important (cf. 21:13).

Notice that the focal point of Paul's entire message and purpose—one that ought to be the same for all preachers and servants of Jesus Christ today—was "the gospel of the grace of God." The apostle's clear emphasis was on grace, God's unmerited favor by which He totally forgives unworthy sinners and freely gives them the complete righteousness of Christ.

The apostle Paul truly walked in the footsteps of faith his entire Christian life and carried out his ministry right to the end. As he approached death, Paul told Timothy, "I have fought the good fight, I have finished the course, I have kept the faith" (2 Tim. 4:7). And when he entered the presence of his Lord, following a ministry of diligent and faithful service, the apostle no doubt heard the comforting words, "Well done, good and faithful slave . . . enter into the joy of your master" (Matt. 25:21).

It should be the goal of all servants of Christ to hear those words from their Master. For us to aim at anything less is unworthy of the Lord who has graciously called us and given us all the spiritual resources we need to honorably serve Him and always glorify His name.

11

LYDIA:

THE GIFT
OF FAITH

In recent decades we have seen the emergence of various so-called liberation movements. Everything from the civil rights movement to liberation theology has promised to free people from oppression and inequality and to elevate them to a better, more just position in society. But no movement that merely rearranges people's economic and social status, without genuinely transforming their hearts, is truly liberating. The only way authentic freedom can be realized is when one's heart is freed from the bondage of sin and death. That's what Jesus meant when He said: "You shall know the truth, and the truth shall make you free" (John 8:32).

The modern women's liberation or feminist movement is another example of a social effort that fails to live up to its extravagant promises of personal freedom and fulfillment. True personal fulfillment comes only through the radical transformation from spiritual death to eternal life, from Satan's realm to God's kingdom, by the divinely initiated work that Scripture calls the new birth. "But as many as received Him, to them He gave the right to become children of God, even to those who believe in His name, who were born not of blood, nor of the will of the flesh, nor of the will of man, but of God" (John 1:12-13; cf. 3:3-8).

Lydia was one New Testament woman who did not need anything such as the feminist movement to feel complete. Instead, as the first recorded Gentile convert in Europe, she was truly a liberated woman, one who came to know the truth of Paul's statement, "The law of the Spirit of life in Christ Jesus has set you free from the law of sin and of death" (Rom. 8:2).

FAITH'S PATH TO LYDIA

The brief story of Lydia is contained in the Acts narrative of the apostle Paul's second missionary journey (which he made with Silas, Timothy, and Luke). After the missionary team visited and taught at many of the churches Paul had previously planted (Acts 15:40-16:5), Paul and his companions were directed by the Holy Spirit to go to Troas. For the time being, all other doors of ministry were closed to them (16:6-8).

In response to Paul's so-called Macedonian vision (Acts 16:9, "Come over to Macedonia and help us"), the missionaries set out for Macedonia (on the Greek mainland), "concluding that God had called us to preach the gospel to them" (v. 10). Luke recorded the details of their route to Macedonia: "Therefore putting out to sea from Troas, we ran a straight course to Samothrace, and on the day following to Neapolis; and from there to Philippi, which is a leading city of the district of Macedonia, a Roman colony; and we were staying in this city for some days" (16:11-12). Philippi was named after Philip II of Macedon (the father of Alexander the Great) and was the eastern terminus of the famous Roman road, the Egnatian Way.

After their initial few days in the city, Paul and his friends sought to carry out his normal evangelistic practice of first preaching in the synagogue of the new locale. (This he did because he would be readily welcomed as a Jewish teacher. And if some Jews were converted to Christ, he would have more help in evangelizing the Gentiles.) But a legitimate synagogue needed at least ten Jewish men who were heads of households, and apparently Philippi's Jewish community was not large enough to form a synagogue. Therefore the missionaries looked for Jews and other God-fearers who gathered in an alternate worship setting. "On the Sabbath day we went outside the gate to a riverside, where we were supposing that there would be a place of prayer" (Acts 16:13).

Paul's team found only women gathered by the river, another indication of how small the Jewish population in Philippi was at that time. The women met to read and discuss the Old Testament Law and to pray. However, they had no man to lead the meeting and teach them. Thus they undoubtedly would have considered it a special privilege to be taught by a traveling rabbi like Paul.

The Spirit-inspired author of Acts, Luke, singled out one of the women: "And a certain woman named Lydia, from the city of Thyatira, a seller of purple fabrics, a worshiper of God, was listening" (Acts 16:14). "Lydia" may not have been her personal name but rather a business name. That's because her home city of Thyatira was in the Roman province of Lydia (hence she may also have been known as "the Lydian lady"). Thyatira, eventually home to one of the seven churches addressed in Revelation (Rev. 2:18-29), manufactured purple dye and dyed goods in ancient times. That kind of dye, which came either from the murex shellfish or the madder plant, was extremely expensive to produce and was used in purple garments worn by royalty and the rich. Therefore the selling of purple fabrics was a very profitable enterprise. Lydia's large house, which had room for the missionaries (Acts 16:15) and the young church at Philippi (v. 40), indicates that she was wealthy.

FAITH'S CAPTURE OF LYDIA'S HEART

There are three noteworthy aspects concerning Lydia's conversion. First, Acts 16:14 describes her as "a worshiper of God," which denotes that she already believed in the God of Israel (but without having become a complete convert to Judaism). That sort of seeking was Lydia's first step toward spiritual liberation. However, like all sinners, she did not really seek God until He sought her. Jesus told the crowd that followed Him, "No one can come to Me, unless the Father who sent Me draws him" (John 6:44; cf. Rom. 3:11).

People sometimes wonder about the eternal fate of those who never hear the Gospel. But Lydia's conversion, like those of Cornelius and the Ethiopian eunuch, demonstrates that God reveals the Gospel to those whom He causes to sincerely seek Him. "All that the Father gives Me shall come to Me, and the one who comes to Me I will certainly not cast out" (John 6:37).

Lydia also "was listening" to the Gospel message Paul preached (Acts 20:14). It is tragic that many today, like Paul's companions on the road to Damascus, hear the sound of preaching but do not actually understand the One who is speaking (Acts 22:9).

Christ sternly told the Jewish leaders why they and others who are hardened to the Gospel often fail to listen to Him:

> *Why do you not understand what I am saying? It is because you cannot hear My word. You are of your father the devil, and you want to do the desires of your father. He was a murderer from the beginning, and does not stand in the truth, because there is no truth in him. Whenever he speaks a lie, he speaks from his own nature; for he is a liar, and the father of lies. But because I speak the truth, you do not believe Me.*
> *—John 8:43-45; cf. Matt. 13:11-17*

But Lydia was not dull of hearing when it came to the truth Paul proclaimed to her and her friends assembled by the river. She listened with faith because "the Lord opened her heart to respond to the things spoken by Paul" (Acts 16:14). Lydia's faith-filled response to the Gospel confirms the truth that God is absolutely sovereign in salvation. That fact had already been powerfully demonstrated during Paul's first missionary journey, at Pisidian Antioch: "when the Gentiles heard this [the gospel], they began rejoicing and glorifying the word of the Lord; and as many as had been appointed to eternal life believed" (Acts 13:48). If God did not open hearts and draw people to Himself, no one would be saved.

FAITH'S REALITY IN LYDIA'S LIFE

After her conversion, Lydia clearly demonstrated that her faith and transformation of heart were genuine. First, she obeyed the Lord's command to be baptized, probably in the river near the place of prayer. The act of baptism shows that a person is identifying with Christ and His people, though it plays no role in bringing one to salvation.

Next, Lydia vigorously ministered hospitality to the missionaries. Luke describes what happened: "She urged us, saying, 'If you have judged me to be faithful to the Lord, come into my house and stay.' And she prevailed upon us" (Acts 16:15).

The practice of Christian hospitality was crucial in the ancient world, where most inns were unfit for believers to stay in. Such places were usually dirty, unsafe, expensive, and often little more than brothels. In those days it was important for Christian women to offer travelers the wholesome alternative of lodging in a Christian home, where they could receive loving treatment and experience godly fellowship and family life (cf. 1 Tim. 5:9-10).

Scripture commands all believers to show hospitality: "Let love of the brethren continue. Do not neglect to show hospitality to strangers, for by this some have entertained angels without knowing it" (Heb. 13:1-2; cf. Matt. 25:34-40; Rom. 12:13; 1 Pet. 4:9). Lydia's earnest offer of hospitality to Paul and his companions was evidence that her new faith was an obedient faith.

Above and beyond her display of hospitality, Lydia is characteristic of all people—men as well as women—who are liberated by having faith in Jesus Christ. And she took that path to spiritual liberation by seeking God, listening to the Gospel, and having a heart that was opened by the Lord so she could respond by faith to the Gospel's message. Anyone who follows Lydia's path will not be disappointed because God promises in Jeremiah 29:13, "You will seek Me and find Me, when you search for Me with all your heart."

12

TIMOTHY:

A FAITHFUL

SPIRITUAL SERVANT

"When a movement develops around a dominant personality," wrote J. Oswald Sanders, "the real test of the quality of his leadership is the manner in which that work survives the crisis of his removal. . . . If he is to discharge his trust fully he will devote time to training younger men to succeed and perhaps even supersede him" (*Spiritual Leadership*, rev. ed. [Chicago: Moody Press, 1980], 210, 217). Every effective leader understands that principle and seeks to implement it in his ministry. Moses handed over Israel's leadership to Joshua, as did David to Solomon. Our Lord spent much of His earthly ministry training the men who would carry on His work. All believers received the truth of the Gospel from those who came before them, and they are responsible to pass that truth on to the next generation. Parents in particular must teach spiritual truth to their children. In Deuteronomy 6:6-9 Moses charged the Israelites to do just that:

> *These words, which I am commanding you today, shall be on your heart; and you shall teach them diligently to your sons and shall talk of them when you sit in your house and when you walk by the way and when you lie down and when you rise up. And you shall bind them as a sign on your hand and they shall be as frontals on your forehead. And you shall write them on the doorposts of your house and on your gates.*

As he neared the end of his life, the apostle Paul, the greatest leader the Christian church has ever known, prepared to pass on his ministry. The last three inspired letters he wrote, those to his disciples Titus and Timothy, were largely concerned with passing the baton of spiritual leadership. Of the countless people he had led to Christ and discipled during his ministry, those two men stood out. Only they did the apostle address with the intimate expression "my true child in the faith" (1 Tim. 1:2; Titus 1:4). Of the two, Timothy most clearly reflected the heart of the apostle. He was Paul's protégé, his spiritual son, and his constant companion in ministry. It was primarily on Timothy that the mantle of Paul's leadership fell (cf. 2 Tim. 2:2).

A YOUNG MAN WELL SPOKEN OF

Timothy grew up in Lystra, a small town in the Roman province of Galatia (part of modern Turkey). His ethnic and religious backgrounds were mixed; his mother was Jewish, and his father was a pagan Greek. Since Timothy had not yet been circumcised when he met Paul (Acts 16:3), he probably had received his formal education in Greek culture. But he also received an education in biblical truth from his devout mother and grandmother (2 Tim. 1:5). Timothy's knowledge of both Greek and Jewish culture made him eminently qualified to accompany Paul on his missionary travels throughout the Greco-Roman world.

Though Acts does not record the details of Timothy's conversion, he, along with his mother and grandmother, was probably converted during Paul's visit to Lystra on the apostle's first missionary journey (Acts 14:6-7). When he revisited Lystra on his second missionary journey, Paul was impressed with Timothy's reputation for godliness (Acts 16:1-2). Despite Timothy's youth (he was probably in his late teens or early twenties), the apostle chose him to replace the deserter John Mark on his missionary team.

The decision to allow Timothy to join Paul must have been a difficult one for Timothy's family. They were well aware of how dangerous traveling with the apostle could be. On his first visit to Lystra, Paul's enemies had stoned him; then, thinking him to be dead, they dumped his bloodied, battered body outside of town (Acts 14:19). Eunice and Lois knew that a similar fate could await Timothy, yet they willingly permitted him to go with Paul. Thus began a close relationship that would last for the rest of Paul's life.

Timothy quickly became Paul's right-hand man. He courageously stayed on in Berea after persecution forced Paul to leave (Acts 17:13-15) and later joined the apostle in Athens. He ministered with Paul in Corinth (Acts 18:5), then was sent by him to Macedonia (Acts 19:22). Timothy traveled with Paul as he set out to return to Jerusalem (Acts 20:4) and was with him when the apostle penned Romans (Rom. 16:21), 2 Corinthians (2 Cor. 1:1), Philippians (Phil. 1:1), Colossians (Col. 1:1), 1 Thessalonians (1 Thess. 1:1), 2 Thessalonians (2 Thess. 1:1), and Philemon (Philem. 1). He went as Paul's representative to the churches at Corinth (1 Cor. 4:17; 16:10; 2 Cor. 1:19), Thessalonica (1 Thess. 3:2), and Philippi (Phil. 2:19).

At the end of Paul's life, Timothy was the pastor of the church at Ephesus (1 Tim. 1:3). In his last inspired writing, the aged apostle, imprisoned and facing imminent execution, urged his beloved friend and coworker to "make every effort to come to me soon" (2 Tim. 4:9). Such was his love for Timothy that Paul longed to see him one last time. Whether Timothy made it to Rome before his beloved mentor's death is unknown.

Little is known for certain of Timothy's later life. Like Paul, he also suffered imprisonment for the cause of Christ; the last reference to him in the New Testament notes his recent release from prison (Heb. 13:23). The details of that imprisonment are not revealed; perhaps he was arrested after visiting Paul in Rome (2 Tim. 4:11, 21; cf. 4:14-15). According to tradition, Timothy suffered martyrdom in the closing years of the first century for opposing the worship of the goddess Diana at Ephesus. Like Paul, Timothy "fought the good fight," "finished the course," and "kept the faith" (2 Tim. 4:7). Since he "[held] fast the beginning of [his] assurance firm until the end" (Heb. 3:14), Timothy is a model of faithfulness for all Christians to follow. From his life and example emerge several principles that should characterize not merely the faith of leaders, but every true servant of Jesus Christ.

A MAN OF PROVEN WORTH

As he prepared to write the letter to the Philippians, the apostle Paul faced a problem. There were some issues in the church at Philippi that desperately needed his personal attention (cf. Phil. 1:27; 2:1; 3:2, 18; 4:2). But unfortunately he was in prison at Rome and unable to go to Philippi. With no other recourse, he decided to send someone in his place. Who would he choose for such an important mission? In Philippians 2:19 Paul wrote, "I hope in the Lord Jesus to send Timothy to you shortly." Timothy was the logical choice since Paul had "no one else of kindred spirit who [would] genuinely be concerned for [their] welfare" (v. 20).

Timothy would reflect Paul's character, communicate Paul's affection, carry Paul's message, and aid the Philippians in their quest for doctrinal clarity, practical unity, and strength to endure persecution. Though the Philippians were well acquainted with Timothy, Paul wanted to make sure they accepted him. Therefore in Philippians 2:20-23, Paul listed seven truths about Timothy that made him eminently qualified to act on Paul's behalf and to be a role model for all Christians today.

Timothy Chose the Right Example

People today, especially young people, have many different role models to choose from. Some pattern their lives after star athletes, others after their favorite actors or actresses, still others after their favorite musicians or teachers. But Timothy chose the best possible model—the apostle Paul. So closely did Timothy follow Paul that he alone was "of kindred spirit" with the apostle (Phil. 2:20). "Kindred spirit" translates a compound word in the Greek, made up of the words for "equal" and "soul." Timothy was one with Paul in mind and spirit; he thought like Paul thought, acted like Paul acted, and felt what Paul felt. In 2 Timothy 3:10 Paul declared that Timothy had "followed my teaching, conduct, purpose, faith, patience, love, perseverance."

The extent to which Timothy was like Paul is remarkable. Paul exhorted the Corinthians to "be imitators of me" (1 Cor. 4:16). Then in verse 17 he added, "For this reason [because I want you to imitate me] I have sent to you Timothy, who is my beloved and faithful child in the Lord, and he will remind you of my ways which are in Christ, just as I teach everywhere in every church." Timothy was such an exact reproduction of Paul that sending him was tantamount to Paul's going himself.

Reproduction is the ultimate goal of discipleship. In Luke 6:40 Jesus said, "Everyone, after he has been fully trained, will be like his teacher." Timothy endeared himself to Paul because he had similar thoughts, qualities, and passions. Therefore the apostle was concerned that he stay on track. His two inspired letters to Timothy are filled with fatherly exhortations (e.g., 1 Tim. 1:3, 18-19; 3:15; 4:6-8, 11-16; 5:21-23; 6:11-14, 20-21; 2 Tim. 1:6, 13-14; 2:1-7, 14-16, 22-26; 3:10, 14). Paul's final exhortation to his beloved son in the faith was especially poignant and powerful:

> *I solemnly charge you in the presence of God and of Christ Jesus, who is to judge the living and the dead, and by His appearing and His kingdom: preach the word; be ready in season and out of season; reprove, rebuke, exhort, with great patience and instruction. For the time will come when they will not endure sound doctrine; but wanting to have their ears tickled, they will accumulate for themselves teachers in accordance to their own desires; and will turn away their ears from the truth, and will turn aside to myths. But you, be sober in all things, endure hardship, do the work of an evangelist, fulfill your ministry.*
>
> *—2 Tim. 4:1-5*

The apostle Paul is the ultimate human role model for believers to follow (cf. 1 Cor. 4:16; 11:1; 1 Thess. 1:6). Certainly no man has had as profound an influence on my own life and ministry as he has.

Paul has provided a model for me not of sinless perfection, like the Lord Jesus Christ, but of a powerful believer, victorious over sin and useful to the Lord. In choosing the apostle Paul as his pattern, Timothy provides an example for all Christians to follow.

Timothy Had a Compassionate Heart

The first specific way in which Timothy was like his mentor was in his sympathetic concern for others. Paul reminded the Philippians that Timothy would "genuinely be concerned for [their] welfare" (2:20). That concern was legitimate, not spurious, hypocritical, or self-serving. Like Paul, Timothy could say, "I do not seek what is yours, but you" (2 Cor. 12:14). He felt the same crushing burden for the welfare of other believers that Paul expressed in 2 Corinthians 11. After listing all the physical suffering he had endured (vv. 23-27), he wrote, "Apart from such external things, there is the daily pressure upon me of concern for all the churches. Who is weak without my being weak? Who is led into sin without my intense concern?" (vv. 28-29). Timothy was a living illustration of what Paul wrote earlier in Philippians 2: "Do nothing from selfishness or empty conceit, but with humility of mind let each of you regard one another as more important than himself; do not merely look out for your own personal interests, but also for the interests of others" (vv. 3-4; cf. Rom. 12:10).

The Greek word translated "concerned" in Philippians 2:20 is commonly rendered "anxious" or "worried." Timothy was greatly burdened for the Philippians' welfare; he felt deeply their hurts and needs. But why did Paul commend Timothy for being anxious when he instructed believers to "be anxious for nothing" (Phil. 4:6), even using the same word translated in this passage as "concerned"? The difference lies in the object of the anxiety. Philippians 4:6 forbids worry and anxiety over one's life circumstances, whereas Philippians 2:20 commands anxious concern for others' spiritual condition and needs.

Timothy's compassion, sympathy, tenderness, and deep concern for the burdens and needs of others should mark all true servants of Jesus Christ.

Timothy Focused on the Right Things

Paul made this point by way of contrast. In Philippians 2:21 he lamented that "all [with him in Rome except Timothy] seek after their own interests, not those of Christ Jesus." They were consumed with their own self-interests; Timothy was consumed with those of Jesus Christ. The self-centeredness of so many of Paul's followers (some of his close companions were no doubt away from Rome ministering elsewhere) is surprising, given the selfless example he set for them. Even his imprisonment wasn't enough to shake them out of their self-centeredness.

There is a tinge of sadness and pathos in Paul's final epistle as he mentions the selfish people who abandoned him in his hour of need. "You are aware of the fact," he wrote to Timothy, "that all who are in Asia turned away from me" (2 Tim. 1:15). Later in that letter Paul noted sadly that "At my first defense no one supported me, but all deserted me," graciously adding, "may it not be counted against them" (2 Tim. 4:16). Perhaps most tragically of all, Paul described how "Demas, having loved this present world, has deserted me and gone to Thessalonica" (2 Tim. 4:10).

Every pastor knows the heartbreak people like Demas cause. Early in my ministry I met regularly with a man for a year, praying with him, discipling him, and counseling him. At the end of that time he left the church, abandoned his family, and denied the faith. Even the Lord Jesus Christ was not immune to such disappointments; when He was arrested, "all the disciples left Him and fled" (Matt. 26:56). And it was one of His apostles, Judas, whose betrayal had led to His arrest.

But Timothy was not like the rest. He alone was a "kindred spirit" to Paul. He alone exhibited that same single-minded devotion to the cause of Christ that characterized the great apostle himself. Sadly, such people are exceptions, but they bring great joy to those with whom they minister. In a church of spectators it is single-minded people like Timothy who make a difference.

Timothy Was a Man of Integrity

Integrity is vital for any Christian and indispensable for a leader. Timothy's integrity was well established; as Paul reminded the Philippians: "You know of his proven worth" (2:22). "Proven worth" translates a Greek word that means "to be approved after testing." Timothy's tests were not academic, but were tests by service, trials, and tribulations.

Timothy's past ministry in Philippi provided unquestionable evidence of his spiritual character and maturity. He had witnessed the birth of the Philippian church (Acts 16:12ff.). Acts 19:22 records that Paul later sent him into Macedonia to minister. Since Philippi was located in Macedonia, Timothy undoubtedly spent much time in that city. The Philippians thus knew firsthand of his proven worth.

Despite his youth, Timothy was a seasoned ministry veteran and the kind of man that the Lord chooses to lead His church. According to 1 Timothy 3:6 an elder must not be "a new convert, lest he become conceited and fall into the condemnation incurred by the devil." Deacons, likewise, must "first be tested; then let them serve as deacons if they are beyond reproach" (1 Tim. 3:10). All believers must, like Timothy, strive to prove their faith in the crucible of everyday living.

Timothy Was Humble

Timothy was the antithesis of those self-centered preachers at Rome who were "preaching Christ even from envy and strife . . . out of selfish ambition, rather than from pure motives, thinking to cause [Paul] distress in [his] imprisonment" (Phil. 1:15, 17). In sharp contrast, he "served with [Paul] in the furtherance of the gospel like a child serving his father" (2:22). Even though he was an apostle and Timothy's spiritual father, Paul's humility kept him from viewing himself as the master and Timothy as the slave. Notice he does not say, "Timothy served me," or "Timothy served under my command," but "he served with me." Timothy's humility caused him to serve Paul with the willing, loving submission of a son who honors and respects his father. The word Paul chooses here for *son* is not the generic term, but a term of endearment meaning "little child."

Timothy would no more have dreamed of competing with Paul than a son would with the father he loves and respects. May God help all Christians to "appreciate those who diligently labor among [them], and have charge over [them] in the Lord and give [them] instruction, and . . . esteem them very highly in love because of their work" (1 Thess. 5:12-13). That will allow those leaders to serve "with joy and not with grief" (Heb. 13:17). Following that important biblical principle could bring healing to many troubled congregations.

Timothy Lived a Life of Sacrifice

"When Christ calls a man," wrote German theologian Dietrich Bonhoeffer, "he bids him come and die. . . . The only man who has the right to say that he is justified by grace alone is the man who has left all to follow Christ" (*The Cost of Discipleship*, rev. ed. [New York: Macmillan, 1977], 7, 55). Timothy was such a man. He understood clearly the significance of Jesus' words, "If anyone wishes to come after Me, let him deny himself, and take up his cross daily, and follow Me" (Luke 9:23). Like any young person, Timothy undoubtedly had plans for his life. Yet he willingly abandoned them all when Paul chose him for ministry. He then devoted the rest of his life to preaching the Gospel of Jesus Christ.

Like many others in the early church, Timothy's sacrifices included prison and martyrdom. Most Christians today are not required to pay such a steep price for their allegiance to Jesus Christ. Yet all of us are called to suffer for our faith. Paul told believers that "Through many tribulations we must enter the kingdom of God" (Acts 14:22). To the Philippians he wrote, "To you it has been granted for Christ's sake, not only to believe in Him, but also to suffer for His sake" (Phil. 1:29). And Paul exhorted Timothy, "Suffer hardship with me, as a good soldier of Christ Jesus" (2 Tim. 2:3).

The pain- and trouble-free Christian life falsely promised by

purveyors of the so-called health and wealth gospel finds no support
in Scripture. Godly men from Job to Jeremiah (the "weeping
prophet") to Jesus Christ ("a man of sorrows, and acquainted with
grief," Isa. 53:3) have experienced pain and suffering. "One son God
hath without sin," wrote Puritan John Trapp, "but none without sorrow" (cited in I. D. E. Thomas, *A Puritan Golden Treasury* [Edinburgh:
Banner of Truth, 1977], 11). Amy Carmichael wrote:

> *Hast thou no scar?*
> *No hidden scar on foot, or side, or hand?*
> *I hear thee sung as mighty in the land,*
> *I hear them hail thy bright ascendant star,*
>   *Hast thou no scar?*
>
>   *Hast thou no wound?*
> *Yet, I was wounded by the archers, spent,*
> *Leaned me against the tree to die; and rent*
> *By ravening beasts that compassed me, I swooned:*
>   *Hast thou no wound?*
>   *No wound? No scar?*
> *Yes, as the Master shall the servant be,*
> *And pierced are the feet that follow Me;*
> *But thine are whole: can he have followed far*
>   *Who has no wound nor scar?*
>   —*Gold Cord* (Fort Washington, Pa.
>   Christian Literature Crusade, 1996), 80

Are you willing, like Timothy, to sacrifice your hopes, your
dreams, and your plans for your Master? Are you willing to accept
His nobler plans?

Timothy Was Available

A man willing to sacrifice all for the cause of Christ will prove eminently useful. Paul noted Timothy's availability when he told the
Philippians, "I hope to send him immediately, as soon as I see how
things go with me" (2:23). That was Timothy, always available, always

willing to be used. At no time in the New Testament accounts did he ever appear to have his own agenda. He was always willing to serve whenever and wherever he was needed.

The constant severing of relationships as he moved from place to place must have been hard for Timothy. In an age without cell phones or E-mail, he would be out of touch with those dear to him for months, even years at a time. But Timothy was not concerned with his own comfort. It didn't matter to him whether he was spending time with those close to him or being thrust into a new situation where he knew no one. All that mattered to him was to fulfill the ministry to which he had been called.

How does your life measure up to Timothy's? Are you well-spoken of by those who know you? Are you a man or woman of proven worth? Whose example do you follow? Where is your focus? Is your life marked by integrity? Are you humble? What have you sacrificed lately for Jesus Christ? Are you available to walk in the footsteps of faith and serve Him wherever, whenever, and however He requires you to?

EPAPHRODITUS:

A MODEL OF

SACRIFICIAL SERVICE

Ever since childhood I've been greatly intrigued by and strongly attracted to the truly sacrificial people of church history. Much of the fascination, I suppose, for me and like-minded individuals who have grown up in modern society is that we see such a contrast between ourselves and the sacrificial lifestyles of other eras. I remember as a young man being profoundly affected by reading about such men as William Carey, Hudson Taylor, David Livingston, and Jim Elliot, who literally gave up their lives for the cause of Christ.

All of those men lived either in another time or served primarily in a setting different from our pampered, affluent culture. And both factors seem to be necessary for us to really appreciate the ministry of sacrifice. We in the West know so little of the sacrificial spirit today that we have to go back to great missionaries of the past or to a New Testament figure such as the often-overlooked servant Epaphroditus.

I believe Epaphroditus is the best scriptural model for a study of sacrificial living because he's the easiest to identify with. John the Baptist, Jesus' disciples, Paul, and Timothy are all great examples of servant-leaders who were called by God and gifted in various ways. They exercised great faith and sacrificed much for the cause of Christ. However, when comparing their lives to our own, the tendency is to conclude, "They are role models worthy of emulating, but they were spiritual giants, and I can't very well identify with that."

But Epaphroditus is a hero of the common man or the average Christian. He was not a statesman or an apostle, and there's no indication he was even an elder in the church at Philippi. His ministry probably did not involve anything dynamic, unforgettable, or earthshaking. Therefore, his sacrificial service is all the more instructive for us, because he ministered faithfully at a level with which most of us are familiar.

We know nothing directly from Scripture about Epaphroditus' background—nothing about his parents, the circumstances of his conversion, or his exact role within the local church. He could have been one of Paul's early converts at Philippi, one who was present when Paul founded that church, but we don't know for sure.

When the New Testament introduces Epaphroditus (Phil. 2:25-30), the apostle Paul was in the midst of his two-year private incarceration at the hands of Rome. The Philippian church was greatly troubled and concerned when it became aware of his situation. Realizing Paul could no longer work and support himself in ministry, church members wanted to send him money. So they collected a sacrificial love-gift and sent it with Epaphroditus to Paul. But Epaphroditus was asked to do more than merely deliver a special offering. The Philippian believers asked him to stay on with Paul and minister to all the apostle's personal needs.

EPAPHRODITUS' BASIC CHARACTER

Epaphroditus' choosing to carry out the Philippian church's special ministry to Paul reveals three important character qualities about him. First, the church would not have sent a man to work closely with Paul if he had not been *the best representative of that congregation's godliness.* The Philippians knew Paul would reject anyone whose character was suspect. Thus Epaphroditus had the highest and truest spiritual virtue and was a man of deep love and commitment to Jesus Christ.

Epaphroditus' mission also indicates he was *a man with a servant's heart.* He was likely a deacon in the church at Philippi and was therefore accustomed to serving others. The Philippians would not have chosen someone who was unwilling to come alongside Paul and sacrifice his life in complete service to the apostle. Otherwise they would have violated their love for Paul and his trust in their good judgment.

Finally, it's clear that Epaphroditus was *a man of great courage* because he knew precisely what risks were involved in going to Paul. He realized that at any time the Romans might execute the imprisoned Paul because the apostle was introducing the "heresy" of Christianity into the Empire. And if they could kill Paul, they could certainly kill those who served alongside him.

PAUL'S TITLES FOR EPAPHRODITUS

In his letter to the Philippians, Paul is more specific in his description of Epaphroditus' character: "I thought it necessary to send to you Epaphroditus, my brother and fellow-worker and fellow-soldier, who is also your messenger and minister to my need" (2:25). Paul ascribes five personal titles to Epaphroditus, three of them concerning the personal relationship between the two men, and two of them concerning Epaphroditus' relationship to the Philippian church.

In Relation to Paul

First of all, Paul gives Epaphroditus the very personal title "my brother." They were brothers in Christ, so they shared the same source of spiritual and eternal life. But the title also conveys the idea of common love. The Greek term for *brother* (*adelphos*) connotes camaraderie, friendship, affection, and good feelings for another. So Paul viewed Epaphroditus not only as a fellow believer, but as a personal friend and comrade.

Paul also refers to Epaphroditus as his "fellow-worker," a term the apostle used many other times to describe people who worked alongside him in ministry and the spreading of the Gospel (cf. Rom. 16:3, 9, 21; Phil. 4:3; 1 Thess. 3:2). So in addition to emphasizing a common spiritual life, Paul states that Epaphroditus engaged in a common ministry with him. By implication Paul commends him for his diligence in helping extend the kingdom of God.

The apostle Paul's third commendation to Epaphroditus in relation to himself is to call him a "fellow-soldier." Paul is using this very honorable Greek title (it was used on special occasions to make the common soldier equal to the commander-in-chief) to elevate Epaphroditus to the level of fellow strategist, fellow commander-in-chief, or fellow leader. The use of this term further indicates that Epaphroditus was engaged alongside Paul in spiritual warfare. They were battling against opponents not only in the earthly, physical realm, but also in the supernatural, spiritual realm.

In Relation to the Philippian Church

Paul continues in Philippians 2:25 to define Epaphroditus' role, now more in relation to the church at Philippi. From the church's viewpoint Epaphroditus was "your messenger," or literally, "your apostle" (*apostolos*). Paul's use of the Greek *apostolos*, however, does not mean Epaphroditus was a uniquely called and dispatched apostle of Christ, as were Paul and the twelve. Here the title is more generic and simply means Epaphroditus was a "messenger" chosen and sent out by the Philippian church.

As indicated earlier, Epaphroditus' initial duty in being a messenger to Paul was to deliver the Philippians' monetary gift. But it's certain that he brought more than money to the apostle. Undoubtedly the church sent along a message of love and a promise that it was praying for Paul. And beyond that, the Philippians considered Epaphroditus their minister to Paul's needs, which is what Epaphroditus' fifth title refers to.

The word translated "minister" (*leitourgon*) referred to priestly religious service and is the term from which we get the English word *liturgy*. The word also referred to the patriotic service rendered by certain citizens of the Greek city-states. Often men, at their own expense, would undertake great civic projects that would benefit their fellow citizens. Those sacrificial public benefactors became known as *leitourgoi*.

Thus Paul's fifth title for Epaphroditus is a fitting one. This remarkable man left his home, family, job, friends, and church and put his life on the line to benefit the apostle Paul. Epaphroditus was the servant-messenger of the Philippian church who came to Paul as the church's minister to help the apostle in every way possible.

EPAPHRODITUS SENT HOME

Paul's fivefold commendation of Epaphroditus to the Philippians is prefaced by the phrase, "I thought it necessary to send to you Epaphroditus" (2:25), followed by the explanation, "because he was longing for you all and was distressed because you had heard that he was sick" (v. 26). In spite of all the good qualities implicit in Paul's titles for his partner in ministry, he found it necessary to send Epaphroditus back to Philippi.

The Reason for His Departure

Superficially, Paul's action is puzzling and causes us to wonder about the reasons for it. But the explanation begins to unfold with his expression "was distressed." The Greek word describes the confused, restless, half-distracted condition produced by severe mental or physical distress. It's the same word Jesus used in Matthew 26:38 to define his state of mind in the Garden of Gethsemane: "My soul is deeply grieved, to the point of death." It denotes a very heavy distress, the kind one commentator says "is the distress that follows a great traumatic shock."

So Epaphroditus was extremely upset, and the reason—"because you had heard that he was sick"-is again difficult for contemporary minds to identify with. This is because our society is much more concerned with material possessions than with personal relationships. We often get very upset about situations and at the same time ignore how people feel.

But that was not true for Epaphroditus. The bond between the Philippians and him was so deep and rich that he was completely stressed out, restless, and saddened because he knew the church at

Philippi was feeling bad about his situation. Therefore Paul felt compelled to send Epaphroditus back to the Philippians. Then Epaphroditus could relieve his own distress by reassuring his much-loved brethren in Philippi that he was all right. Otherwise Paul knew his fellow-worker would not have sufficient peace of mind to be able to continue helping him in the ministry.

What was the exact nature of Epaphroditus' difficulty? Paul characterized it as "sick to the point of death" (Phil. 2:27) and "he came close to death for the work of Christ" (v. 30). The apostle does not explain the affliction beyond those phrases. I do think we can infer that Epaphroditus was facing a traumatic situation, serious enough that God's mercy was needed to deliver him from it. Also, the word rendered "sick" in verse 27 primarily means "weakness." It was the same kind of weakness Paul mentions elsewhere in relation to himself: "Therefore I am well content with weaknesses, with insults, with distresses, with persecutions, with difficulties, for Christ's sake; for when I am weak, then I am strong" (2 Cor. 12:10). It is the kind of weakness that results from making oneself vulnerable to a hostile, godless, persecuting environment.

But why would anyone want to place himself in such a difficult, stressful, and exhausting position, even for the sake of Christ? Epaphroditus was more than willing to do so because of his sacrificial character. Paul explains that he was "risking his life to complete what was deficient in your service to me" (Phil. 2:30). He uses an interesting Greek verb (*paraboleusamenos*) for "risking," literally meaning, "to roll the dice." The idea is that Epaphroditus was willing to gamble with his own comfort and security, to expose himself to whatever dangers arose as he ministered for Paul. Epaphroditus was so loyal, faithful, humble, uncomplaining, and sacrificial that he put his life on the line to serve Paul on behalf of the Philippians. He loved Jesus Christ, the apostle Paul, and his brethren at Philippi much more than he loved himself. He was suffering in his ministry for Paul and doubly in his concern for his beloved church.

The Reception He Was Due

Although Epaphroditus would have humbly played down the idea, Paul was convinced that his fellow-worker's self-sacrificing service for the cause of Christ and on behalf of others was worthy of great respect. The apostle thus urged the Philippians to give Epaphroditus the proper reception on his return to them: "Therefore receive him in the Lord with all joy, and hold men like him in high regard" (Phil. 2:29).

The word "receive" means "to welcome, to embrace, to take in." Romans 15:7 (KJV) says, "Wherefore receive ye one another, as Christ also received us, to the glory of God." Paul wanted the church at Philippi to rejoice that Epaphroditus had returned healthy. The believers were not to regard his return as an indication of failure, but to respect him as a precious, honorable man, one whom the church should cherish as a highly prized brother.

The entire account of Epaphroditus, Paul, and the Philippian church exemplifies the highest standards of Christian love, sympathy, unselfish concern, and the desire to comfort someone at the expense of personal preferences. The Philippians weren't demanding the return of Epaphroditus; they were in the midst of their own trials (Phil. 1:29). Paul had his own trial of imprisonment. And Epaphroditus had risked death in his ministry for and with Paul.

But in spite of all those difficulties, the Philippians were concerned for Epaphroditus, Epaphroditus was concerned for the Philippians, and Paul was concerned for both. This is a practical illustration of the apostle's admonitions earlier, in Philippians 2:

> *Do nothing from selfishness or empty conceit, but with humility of mind let each of you regard one another as more important than himself; do not merely look out for your own personal interests, but also for the interests of others.*
>
> *—vv. 3-4*

*Work out your salvation with fear and trembling; for it is God
who is at work in you, both to will and to work for His good pleasure. Do all things without grumbling or disputing.*

—*vv. 12-14*

Among all the ordinary believers who are mentioned in the New
Testament, there is hardly a better example of a life of sacrificial service than that of Epaphroditus. He humbly served the cause of Jesus
Christ without expecting to receive public accolades. He was not
head and shoulders above others like the apostle Paul. Epaphroditus
did not have the kind of preeminent, Spirit-endowed gifts of teaching, preaching, and leadership that Timothy had. Instead, he was an
average, behind-the-scenes, faithful and compassionate believer.

In that sense his example ought to apply all the more directly to each
one of us who wants to walk in the footsteps of faith daily. There are very
few Pauls, some Timothys, but there can be many Epaphrodituses.

14

JESUS CHRIST:

THE ULTIMATE

EXAMPLE OF FAITH

===

The judicious use of metaphors is an important aspect of effective teaching, and the biblical writers used them to great effect. In fact, the New Testament frequently compares the Christian life to the common activities of life.

The apostle Paul was particularly fond of using the metaphor of a race. For example, he writes, "Do you not know that those who run in a race all run, but only one receives the prize? Run in such a way that you may win" (1 Cor. 9:24), "You were running well" (Gal. 5:7), and, "I did not run in vain" (Phil. 2:16).

The writer of Hebrews also used that metaphor as he likened faithful life in Christ to a race (12:1-3). But this isn't like any race run by world-class athletes. Those who have put their faith in Christ are runners who can certainly experience victory. Unfortunately, too many believers run the race indifferently, either not putting forth the necessary effort to be successful or, even worse, hardly running at all.

In the previous chapters of this book we have examined the lives of several faithful servants of our Lord, some of whom the author of Hebrews included in his Hall of Faith (Heb. 11). In Hebrews 12:1-3 the writer uses the running metaphor to motivate believers—and those who had made a profession of faith—to follow in the footsteps of those who had gone before them. He encourages us to run the faith race with endurance and excellence, to eliminate hindrances to running, to set our sights on the goal, and to look forward to the fruits of victory awaiting us at the finish.

FOLLOWING THE EXAMPLES OF FAITH

The author begins by referring back to the faithful saints of Hebrews 11: "Therefore, since we have so great a cloud of witnesses surrounding us . . ." (12:1). Anyone entering a race wants to perform well—he wants to know that he has a legitimate chance of winning. Otherwise, why put forth the effort? Fortunately, the great believers from the past who lived the life of faith are our motivation and encouragement. We are to run the race of faith like they did—always trusting, never giving up, no matter what the obstacles or hardships or cost—and thus being blessed by God.

They knew how to run the race of faith. The writer of Hebrews explained how Moses opposed Pharaoh, abandoned the pleasures and privileges of his court, and then passed through the Red Sea (11:24-29). He described how others were tortured, mocked, scourged, imprisoned, stoned, and so on, all for the sake of their faith (vv. 37-39). In this book we have looked at how certain Old and New Testament saints overcame great trials.

In 12:1 the "cloud of witnesses surrounding us" is not made up of spectators cheering us on in the race; the witnesses are our historic spiritual examples, their lives testifying that the life of faith is the only life to live. They have run the race and are witnesses to the victory that God will give us at the end.

Nothing is more encouraging than the successful example of someone who has gone before us. Because they have done it, they serve to motivate us to run like they did. And to know that God was with them encourages us to trust that He will also be with us. Their God is our God. We have the same God, and He can bring the same blessing to us if we trust Him. That is our motivation to run the race of faith.

RUNNING THE RACE OF FAITH

How are we to run this race of faith? The author of Hebrews says, "Let us run with endurance the race that is set before us" (12:1). He is telling us to run with endurance—to not give up.

Unfortunately, as I said before, many Christians could hardly be described as running the race at all. Some are jogging, some are walking, and some are barely moving. Yet, the biblical standard for holy living is a race, not a walk in the park.

The Greek word for race is *agon*, from which we get the English word *agony*. It is an agonizing effort; it is demanding and grueling and requires total commitment to self-discipline, determination, and perseverance. That's why God warned Israel, "Woe to those who are at ease in Zion, and to those who feel secure in the mountain of Samaria" (Amos 6:1). In God's army we never hear, "At ease." To stand still or to go backwards is to forfeit the prize.

"Run with Endurance"

To "run with *endurance*" means to keep running when everything in you wants to slow down or give up. I can still remember the first time I ran the half-mile in high school. I usually ran the 100-yard dash, which requires a quick burst of speed only. So I started out well in the half-mile; in fact I led the pack for the first 100 yards or so. But I ended up dead last, and I felt like I was dead. My legs were wobbly, I was completely out of breath, and I collapsed at the finish line. That's the way many believers live the Christian life. They start out fast, but, undisciplined and adrift spiritually, they soon encounter obstacles or impediments, slow down, give up, or just collapse. You must understand that the Christian race is a marathon, not a sprint. To win a marathon, you must be disciplined to endure weariness and exhaustion. The same is true in the Christian life.

The Philippians needed to understand that, so Paul wrote, "Prove yourselves to be blameless and innocent, children of God above reproach in the midst of a crooked and perverse generation, among whom you appear as lights in the world" (Phil. 2:15). "Do you not know that those who run in a race all run, but only one receives the prize? Run in such a way that you may win. And everyone who competes in the games exercises self-control in all things. They then do it to receive a perishable wreath, but we an imperishable" (1 Cor. 9:24-25).

Run with Excellence

Nothing is more disturbing than to see Christians who have little desire to win. Yet I believe the lack of desire to win is a basic problem with many believers. They are content simply to be saved and to wait to go to heaven. But that's unacceptable in the Christian life.

If you claim allegiance to Jesus Christ as your Lord, you need to strive for as much excellence as you can in every endeavor. If you're a Sunday school teacher, be the most excellent teacher you can be. If you're a Bible study leader, lead your flock with excellence. If you're a homemaker, make your home as excellent as it can be. When you're at your job, do the most excellent work you can. That's the only way to live the Christian life. It takes discipline, but we must demand excellence of ourselves and run the race to win.

Paul believed that principle. He didn't pursue comfort, wealth, popularity, respect, position, or anything else but only God's will. He said, "Therefore I run in such a way, as not without aim; I box in such a way, as not beating the air; but I buffet my body and make it my slave, lest possibly, after I have preached to others, I myself should be disqualified" (1 Cor. 9:26-27). That's what Christian commitment is all about.

The only way you can possibly endure as a Christian is by faith. Failure to endure is a failure to trust the Lord. Only as you use "the shield of faith" (Eph. 6:16) can you withstand Satan's temptations. When you trust and obey God-when you run in the power of God's Spirit—Satan and sin have no power over you.

MAXIMIZING YOUR POTENTIAL IN THE RACE

The writer of Hebrews continues his race metaphor by exhorting, "Let us also lay aside every encumbrance" (12:1). An "encumbrance" is simply a bulk or mass. One major problem runners have to deal with is weight. Christians also have a weight problem. Whatever weighs us down diverts our attention, saps our energy, and dampens our enthusiasm for God's will. Just as a runner can't win when he carries excess weight, neither can we.

In most sports, especially where speed and endurance are critical, weighing in is a daily routine. It is one of the simplest, yet most reliable tests of one's physical condition. When an athlete exceeds his weight limit, he must exercise and adhere to a stricter diet until he loses the unwanted pounds.

Too much clothing is also a hindrance. When the race begins, athletes run with the least clothing that decency allows. They can't afford to be concerned about how they look. Unfortunately, many Christians are more concerned about appearance than about spiritual reality. As a result, they seriously hamper their testimony for Jesus Christ.

Eliminate Self-Righteousness

We don't know for sure what spiritual encumbrances the writer of Hebrews was referring to, but the context leads me to believe the main problem was Judaistic legalism. Dead works characterized many Jewish believers. The ceremonies, rituals, and rules of Judaism were no longer of any value, since their purpose was to point to Christ. He was the new reality to spiritual living, and the ceremonies became hindrances when they diverted people away from Christ. The Jewish believers or would-be believers could not possibly run the Christian race if they were carrying all that excess baggage.

Some in the Galatian churches faced the same problem. Paul said, "I have been crucified with Christ; and it is no longer I who live, but Christ lives in me; and the life which I now live in the flesh I live by faith in the Son of God, who loved me, and delivered Himself up for me. I do not nullify the grace of God; for if righteousness comes through the Law, then Christ died needlessly" (Gal. 2:20-21). He also said, "You foolish Galatians, who has bewitched you, before whose eyes Jesus Christ was publicly portrayed as crucified? This is the only thing I want to find out from you: did you receive the Spirit by the works of the Law, or by hearing with faith? Are you so foolish? Having begun by the Spirit, are you now being perfected by the flesh?" (3:1-3). To make his point even more clear, Paul said, "But now that you have come to know God, or rather to be known by God, how is it that you turn back again to the weak and worthless elemental things, to which you desire to be enslaved all over again?" (4:9). Once you begin to run the Christian race, there is no need to be encumbered by old clothes.

Eliminate Sin

An even more significant hindrance to Christian living is sin: "Let us also lay aside . . . the sin which so easily entangles us" (12:1). The use of the definite article before "sin" may indicate particular sins. And one specific sin that most commonly hinders the race of faith is unbelief, or doubting God. You can't doubt and live in faith at the same time—they are contradictions. Unbelief "entangles" our feet, tripping us up so that we cannot run effectively. The writer adds that sin "easily entangles us." When we let sin rule in our lives, especially unbelief, we make it easy for Satan to cause us to stumble in our pursuit of the Lord.

FOCUSING ON THE GOAL OF THE RACE

How do you keep from stumbling in the race? When you run, where you look is important. Nothing will throw you off your stride or slow you down like looking at your feet or the other runners in the race. Since the same is true in the Christian race, the writer of Hebrews says we should be "fixing our eyes on Jesus, the author and perfecter of faith, who for the joy set before Him endured the cross, despising the shame, and has sat down at the right hand of the throne of God" (12:2).

Because we live in a society that elevates self, it is easy for most believers to become preoccupied with themselves. Most are not selfish or egotistical, but they're inordinately focused on what they're doing—on how they should or shouldn't be living the Christian life. Obviously we need to examine ourselves in that regard (2 Cor. 13:5); but if we become preoccupied with ourselves, we will never run well for the Lord. Concern for others is also important, but if our focus is on them, we will also stumble. We shouldn't even focus on the Holy Spirit. Instead, we are to be filled with the Spirit, and when we are, we will focus on Jesus Christ, because the Spirit focuses on Him (John 16:14). When our focus is on Christ, we will have His perspective on ourselves and on others.

The Author of Faith

We are to focus on Jesus because He is "the author . . . of faith" (Heb. 12:2). That means He is the originator or pioneer, the one who begins and takes the lead.

As the originator of all faith, Jesus originated Noah's faith, Abraham's faith, Paul's faith, and our faith. Paul said, "Our fathers . . . all ate the same spiritual food; and all drank the same spiritual drink, for they were drinking from a spiritual rock which followed them; and the rock was Christ" (1 Cor. 10:1, 3-4).

But I believe the primary meaning of "author" in Hebrews 12:2 is "chief leader" or "chief example." Jesus Christ is our preeminent example of faith. He was "tempted in all things as we are, yet without sin" (Heb. 4:15). When the devil tempted Him in the wilderness, Jesus trusted in God and His Word. He didn't circumvent His Father's will just to get food, or test His Father's protection and lordship (Matt. 4:1-10). He waited on God to meet His needs. Jesus trusted Him for everything and in everything: "I can do nothing on My own initiative. As I hear, I judge; and My judgment is just, because I do not seek My own will, but the will of Him who sent Me" (John 5:30).

In the Garden of Gethsemane, just before His arrest, trial, and crucifixion, Jesus said to His Father, "My Father, if it is possible, let this cup pass from Me; yet not as I will, but as Thou wilt" (Matt. 26:39). Jesus knew He was about to face the most severe suffering of His human life; yet He trusted His Father's will. To follow in our Lord's footsteps, we must try to match His commitment of faith in God's will.

The Perfecter of Faith

As the *"perfecter* of faith," Jesus carries it through to completion. He perfectly trusted His Father right up to the moment of His death when He said, "It is finished!" (John 19:30) and "Father, into Thy hands I commit My spirit" (Luke 23:46). But He did more than just finish His work—He perfected it. He accomplished exactly what He meant to accomplish. From His birth to His death, Jesus was totally committed to accomplishing His Father's will, which was to provide salvation through His Son's death and resurrection. In faith He "endured the cross, despising the shame" (Heb. 12:2). Why should we not too trust God in everything since we have not begun to suffer what Jesus suffered? "You have not yet resisted to the point of shedding blood in your striving against sin" (v. 4).

The great men and women we have studied in the previous chapters are wonderful models of faith, but none of them has matched Jesus' perfect walk of faith. Because He has set such a high example of faith, we should fix our eyes on Him for as long as we live (cf. 2 Cor. 3:18).

ENJOYING THE FRUITS OF VICTORY

No one would run a marathon without some expectation of reward. And the same is true of the race of faith—if you don't have something to look forward to at the end of it, you'll likely never start it, let alone finish it. So the writer of Hebrews encourages us with the outcome of Jesus' faith: "who for the joy set before Him endured the cross, despising the shame, and has sat down at the right hand of the throne of God" (12:2).

Jesus did not run His race of faith for the pleasure of the experience only. Certainly our Lord experienced great pleasure in healing, comforting, encouraging, and saving people. But He didn't leave His Father's presence and heavenly glory, endure temptation and hostility by Satan, suffer blasphemy and crucifixion at the hands of his enemies, and tolerate misunderstanding and denial by His disciples for the sake of the pleasures He had while on earth. He was motivated by much more than that.

Only what awaited Him at the end of His earthly ministry could have motivated Jesus to leave and endure what He did. Two things motivated Jesus: "the joy set before Him" and sitting "down at the right hand of the throne of God." Jesus ran the race of faith for the joy of exaltation. In His high-priestly prayer Jesus said to His Father, "I glorified Thee on the earth, having accomplished the work which Thou hast given Me to do. And now, glorify Thou Me together with Thyself, Father, with the glory which I ever had with Thee before the world was" (John 17:4-5). Jesus glorified God on earth by displaying the Father's attributes and completing His Father's will.

We run for the same reason Jesus did, and we achieve victory in the same way. We run for the joy of exaltation that God promises will be ours if we glorify Him on earth. By following our Lord's example, we glorify God by allowing His attributes to shine through us and by obeying His will in everything we do.

But we can also experience joy now as we anticipate the heavenly reward of our faithful service. Paul's converts were his "joy and crown" (Phil. 4:1) and his "hope or joy or crown of exultation" (1 Thess. 2:19). The people he led to salvation in Christ were evidence that he had glorified God in his ministry.

The reward at the end thus becomes our motivation to forget "what lies behind and [reach] forward to what lies ahead," pressing on "toward the goal of the prize of the upward call of God in Christ Jesus" (Phil. 3:13-14). "In the future," the apostle says, "there is laid up for me the crown of righteousness, which the Lord, the righteous Judge, will award to me on that day; and not only to me, but also to all who have loved His appearing" (2 Tim. 4:8). When we get to heaven, we can join the twenty-four elders in casting our "crowns before the throne, saying, 'Worthy art Thou, our Lord and our God, to receive glory and honor and power'" (Rev. 4:10-11).

As we run the race of the Christian life and follow in the footsteps of the great men and women of faith, we can joyfully look forward to receiving the crown of righteousness, which we will cast at our Lord's feet as proof of our eternal love for Him.

STUDY

GUIDE

CHAPTER 1:
NOAH: A FAITH THAT OBEYS

Summarizing the Chapter

Noah's obedient and persevering life is a lasting illustration of the kind of faith that rebukes the world and proves what a genuine relationship with God is like.

Getting Started (Choose One)

1. What contemporary social evils or problems (street gangs, legalized abortion, child abuse, school violence, others) remind you most of the days before the Flood? Are today's problems worse than problems then? Why or why not?

2. What situation in your Christian life has been most challenging for you in exercising obedient faith? How has the experience helped strengthen your walk with God?

Answering the Questions

1. What two extreme, opposite, and wrong viewpoints does Satan promote regarding the relationship between faith and works?

2. What does Genesis 5:28-32 indicate about Noah's relationship to his ancestors?

3. How and why did Noah find favor with God (see the quotation from James Montgomery Boice's commentary)?

4. What factors were potential hindrances to Noah's prompt obedience in building the ark?

5. In one sentence, what does the ark symbolize?

6. What did God do with the faith of Noah and Abraham (Gen. 15:6; Rom. 4:3; Heb. 11:7)?

7. What sort of activity in Noah's time brought an end to God's perfectly holy patience?

8. Why is it astounding that no one responded to Noah's preaching?

9. What are we forced to conclude when comparing pre-Flood days with today?

Focusing on Prayer

• Ask God to give you the kind of godly perseverance with your daily tasks that Noah had when building the ark and warning the people around him.

• Spend some extra time this week praying for your community. Ask God to draw some people from the grip of rampant sin and toward the truth of the Gospel.

Applying the Truth

Read the entire account of the Flood (Gen. 6:1-9:17). Keep a written record of the many times and various ways Noah exhibited faith and obedience. Share your most meaningful insights with someone in a way that would encourage him or her to trust God like Noah did.

CHAPTER 2:
ABRAHAM: A PATTERN OF FAITH

Summarizing the Chapter

Abraham's life followed a complete pattern of faith and is a prototype for anyone today who wants saving faith.

Getting Started (Choose One)

1. What ceremonies and laws do people commonly point to in hopes of justifying their spiritual well-being? How easy is it to show them the inadequacy of such hopes? What's the most unusual such hope ever shared with you?

2. How difficult is it for most people to move to a new community far from their hometown? If you have had that experience, what did you find most helpful in getting adjusted?

Answering the Questions

1. Where did Abraham originally live? What kind of city was it?

2. What did God promise Abraham as he was leaving his homeland?

3. What two major failings did Abraham's faith endure after he left home? What were the consequences?

4. What major test of faith is Abraham best known for passing?

5. Why did Abraham need patience throughout his pilgrimage? What made him successful?

6. What does the Greek word for "reckoned" mean (Rom. 4:5)? How is this concept related to the doctrine of justification (vv. 3-4)?

7. How should circumcision be understood within the covenant relationship between God and the Jews?

8. Demonstrate how a simple Old Testament chronology proves that Abraham was not justified by keeping the law.

9. What four key elements are found in God's covenant promise to Abraham?

10. How does faith differ from hope? What was the object of Abraham's faith?

11. Name at least three other aspects of Abraham's faith. What are some Scripture references that support these?

Focusing on Prayer

- Thank the Lord that He sovereignly called Abraham out of a pagan environment and made him the father of faith for the rest of us.
- Pray through the six God-given features of Abraham's faith, and ask the Lord to make them true in your life as well.

Applying the Truth

Memorize Romans 4:3-5 or Hebrews 11:8.

CHAPTER 3:
MOSES: A LIFE OF GODLY CHOICES

Summarizing the Chapter

Moses is a superior example of how to apply faith in consistently selecting God's way over the world's.

Getting Started (Choose One)

1. All of us often associate particular people and personalities with certain ideas or events. What people in your life do you match up in this way? Why?

2. What from the world's system has most often been a source of enticement or distraction for you? What are some ways you have learned to resist and overcome this particular temptation?

Answering the Questions

1. Is it accurate to call Moses a legalist? Why or why not?

2. What occurred in Egypt that placed baby Moses' life in jeopardy? What did his parents and sister do to protect him?

3. What faith-strengthening truths did Moses' mother teach him?

4. What was Egypt's national status while Moses was growing up?

5. Compare and contrast Moses' experience in Egypt with that of Joseph.

6. What has modern archaeology verified about Egypt during Moses' time?

7. Briefly explain how and why Moses suffered for Christ (see Heb. 11:25-26).

8. What was the biggest intimidation Moses had to deal with?

9. What was the purpose of the first Passover? Did Moses and the people understand its full meaning?

10. What was the only guarantee of deliverance the Israelites had at the edge of the Red Sea?

Focusing on Prayer

• Pray that God would help you to be faithful every day in making scriptural choices.

• Ask God for wisdom and faithfulness to bring up your children according to His plan. If you have no children, pray for the children of relatives and friends.

Applying the Truth

Identify a personal possession or attitude that has hindered you from following the Lord as you should. Prayerfully resolve, like Moses, to forsake that hindrance and replace it with God's choice for your life. Jot down some specific steps that could help you achieve your goal. Also write out a verse such as Romans 8:18 or 2 Corinthians 4:17 for memorization and meditation.

CHAPTER 4:
RAHAB: DISTINCTIVE FAITH

Summarizing the Chapter

God saves those who truly believe, such as Rahab, even if He must judge all the sinners around them, such as the people of Jericho.

Getting Started (Choose One)

1. How important is a good church and family environment in one's coming to saving faith? In what ways might these advantages actually keep a young person from coming to genuine faith? Discuss.

2. Is complete honesty always the best policy? Why or why not? In what circumstances might it be right to withhold certain information? Have you ever faced such a difficult decision?

Answering the Questions

1. Why is Rahab at first glance an unlikely candidate for inclusion in this book? What two facts make studying her life worthwhile?

2. What was the main purpose for Joshua's sending spies to Jericho? Why did he send them secretly?

3. Why was Jericho's king so upset and frightened at discovering the spies?

4. What were the two reasons Rahab had no qualms about lying to protect the spies?

5. In addition to rescue from Jericho's destruction, what does the red cord in Rahab's window signify?

6. How did Rahab prove the genuineness of her faith?

Focusing on Prayer

•   Perhaps you know someone for whose salvation you've stopped praying because he or she seems so unlikely to respond to the Gospel. Rahab's salvation says we ought to keep praying for such people. If you know of someone like this, don't stop interceding for him or her.

•   Thank the Lord that He providentially arranges help and direction for those in need, as He did with the two spies.

Applying the Truth

Extend hospitality or an offer of service to someone you know. Ideally this should be to a person or family member who has definite needs. Ask God to make the opportunity more than just a time of sharing a meal or doing a favor for others.

CHAPTER 5:
HANNAH: THE FAITHFUL MOTHER

Summarizing the Chapter

Hannah, through her right relationships with husband, God, and home, is a role model of the faithful and godly mother.

Getting Started (Choose One)

1. Rearing children is a noble calling, but not everyone will have the opportunity. Have some members of your group who do not have children share ways God has allowed them to minister to others' children.

2. What is the longest amount of time you can recall praying for something? What was it, and how did you respond when God finally answered?

Answering the Questions

1. List three of the five women other than Hannah who are given as examples of godly women and mothers.

2. During what time in Israel's history did Hannah live? What did the nation need most then?

3. What ancient practice created difficulty for Hannah's marriage?

4. How would you characterize the spiritual maturity of Elkanah? How did he demonstrate that?

5. What was the significance of the double portion Elkanah gave to Hannah?

6. How did Elkanah react to the difficulty between Hannah and Peninnah?

7. What was Hannah's primary motive in wanting a son?

8. What was the distinctive virtue of Hannah's prayer life?

9. What is the last part of Hannah's promise in 1 Samuel 1:11 called? What did it involve?

10. What did Eli the high priest misunderstand about Hannah's prayer actions in the temple?

11. What did the Old Testament expression "worthless woman" connote?

12. How does patient prayer-faith like Hannah's reveal itself?

13. What passage can Hannah's words of praise in 1 Samuel 2:1-10 be likened to?

14. What child-rearing principle was Hannah committed to (see 1 Sam. 1:21-23; Deut. 6:6-9)? How does that compare to many mothers' attitudes today?

Focusing on Prayer

• Thank the Lord for the well-rounded example of godliness and faithfulness that Hannah provides.
• Pray for someone who may be struggling with marital or parenting issues. Ask that he or she might turn his or her problem over to God like Hannah did.

Applying the Truth

Read and meditate on Deuteronomy 6:6-9. Identify the principles for teaching the Word to your children, and plan practical ways you can implement them, either with your children or with those at your church who need a spiritual mentor.

CHAPTER 6:
JONAH: THE RELUCTANT MISSIONARY

Summarizing the Chapter

Through its teaching about his sinful attitude and motive for ministry, Jonah's story illustrates the consequences of a believer's disobedience and unfaithfulness to the Lord's call to ministry.

Getting Started (Choose One)

1. Does the story of Jonah prove or disprove the theory that trials and sufferings come to a believer only because of sin in his life? Discuss the group's various answers, including your own.

2. What is your most frequently expressed opinion of people such as liberals, pro-abortionists, extreme environmentalists, or homosexual activists (the so-called gay rights movement)? Do you ever consider that some of them—even one—could be saved? What is the best way to pray for them?

Answering the Questions

1. What was the twofold ministry of the Old Testament prophets?

2. What is the main lesson we can learn from Jonah's primarily negative example?

3. What other well-known prophet did Jonah likely know and serve under (2 Kings 6:1-7)?

4. What were the chief physical characteristics of Nineveh? The spiritual characteristics of its people?

5. What sinful attitudes in Israel did God end up reproving through Jonah?

6. Give the reasons for Jonah's blatantly disobedient response to God's first missionary commission of him.

7. What was the deeper issue behind Jonah's initial rebellion? Elaborate briefly.

8. What should Jonah's running the other way teach us about God's presence and our availability to Him (see Ps. 139:7-9)?

9. What does Jonah 1:4-16 suggest about sin's relationship to natural disasters?

10. How did God minister to the pagan sailors during and after the storm? Why was Jonah so useless at that time?

11. What two lessons did Jonah learn as he repented inside the fish?

12. What happened as a result of Jonah's obedient preaching in Nineveh? How does that event compare in scope with similar occurrences later in redemptive history?

13. How did Jonah respond to what God did in Nineveh? What continuing attitude did his reaction reveal?

14. What was God's final lesson for Jonah?

Focusing on Prayer

• Pray that God would guard you from any attitudes of religious or ethnic pride. Confess any such thoughts that His Spirit may bring to your mind.

• Thank God for His grace, mercy, and forgiving heart that often gives us second chances to serve Him.

Applying the Truth

Carefully read through and meditate on Psalm 139. Make note of the various ways it describes God's omnipresence and His intimate knowledge of each believer. Memorize several verses that might strengthen you as you talk to someone with whom you should have shared God's Word a long time ago.

CHAPTER 7:
MARY: A FAITHFUL WORSHIPER OF GOD

Summarizing the Chapter

To a contemporary church that has largely abandoned biblical worship, Mary the mother of Jesus is a model of sincere, unquestioning, worshipful faith.

Getting Started (Choose One)

1. How scriptural do you feel the worship is at your church? What aspect of the worship there do you like best? What would you change? Use specific examples.

2. Would you consider yourself essentially a grateful person? What is the key ingredient of personal thankfulness? What do you think is the most common obstacle to it? Why?

Answering the Questions

1. What are the essentials of the Roman Catholic portrayal of Mary?

2. What reality is important to know about Mary's general background?

3. What elements in Luke 1:26-38 indicate the unusual nature of Mary's experience?

4. What is the definition and significance of the *kiddushin*?

5. Why might Mary have doubted that the angel's announcement was good news (see Matt. 1:19)?

6. What are the four aspects of Mary's attitude of true worship?

7. What was the object of Mary's worship, and why was she so eager to acknowledge it?

8. What are the three basic reasons Mary worshiped the Lord so fervently?

9. How can we know that Mary, for all her words, was in no way building herself up (see Luke 1:48-49)?

Focusing on Prayer

• Thank the Lord for Mary's faithfulness and obedience in being the mother of the Savior.
• Pray that your church would always honor God with true, heartfelt worship. If the church does not follow Scripture in certain aspects of worship, pray specifically about those.

Applying the Truth

Music and singing are vital parts of any good worship service. Spend some time with your hymnal (or one borrowed from your church), and meditate on the words of the more worshipful hymns. Make a list of those you

see as best for encouraging a true spirit of worship. Focus especially on
ones you are less familiar with.

CHAPTER 8:
JOHN THE BAPTIST: THE GREATEST MAN

Summarizing the Chapter

John the Baptist, because of his personal character, privileged calling, and
powerful culmination, is an ideal pattern for all believers who seek true
greatness in Christ's kingdom.

Getting Started (Choose One)

1. At the end of this century experts have compiled various lists of the
   greatest movies, novels, news events, and so forth. Who would you
   choose as the greatest or most influential person of the twentieth century? Explain why.

2. The easy way always seems to be the most popular, most accepted
   way to do things in society. In what areas is that especially true? When
   are you most tempted to cut corners or be less disciplined?

Answering the Questions

1. What kind of family did John come from? What did his father do?

2. How was John destined for greatness? What was to be his primary
   ministry task?

3. What did Jesus say so people would not misunderstand the nature of
   John's greatness (Matt. 11:11)?

4. What factors helped John overcome certain weaknesses?

5. Regarding John's strong convictions, what commonplace item did
   Jesus ask the people to contrast them with? Why was that illustration
   appropriate?

6. Describe John's food and dress. What did his lifestyle rebuke?

7. What title did this chapter use for John in relation to the Old Testament prophets? What was his prophetic style?

8. What is the one word that summarizes John's message? Briefly, what all did that involve?

9. What was the twofold duty of the royal herald? How did John accomplish that for the spiritual needs of the people?

10. Contrast John's baptism to the Levitical washings.

11. What kind of reaction did John's message typically provoke?

12. In what respect was John a culmination?

13. What was Jesus' point in comparing John to Elijah (Matt. 11:14)?

14. What six facts demonstrate John's true greatness?

Focusing on Prayer

• Praise and thank God that in terms of spiritual inheritance you are as great as John the Baptist.
• Pray for someone you know who needs to hear strong preaching like John would deliver—whether a believer in a weak church or an unbeliever.

Applying the Truth

Memorize Isaiah 40:3-5. Meditate on it and review it, especially when you struggle with a particular obstacle or piece of rough terrain in your walk with the Lord. Ask Him for practical ways to make your path smooth.

CHAPTER 9:
PETER: LESSONS LEARNED BY FAITH

Summarizing the Chapter

Our Lord used various blessings, corrections, and learning experiences in the life of Peter to transform him from a proud and unpolished fisherman into a faithful leader of the apostles and an effective teacher and author of Scripture.

Getting Started (Choose One)

1. What do you recall as the most difficult lesson you've ever learned? Why are you glad you had the experience?

2. What qualities of leadership do you appreciate most? In what person or persons have you seen those best exemplified? In what ways did that person help you?

Answering the Questions

1. What does the Greek in Matthew 10:2 say about Peter's position among the disciples?

2. What was Peter's name changed from? What does Peter ("Cephas") mean in Aramaic, and how is that indicative of the character quality Jesus wanted for him?

3. Where was Peter's hometown? Where did he have his fishing business?

4. What kinds of questions did Peter ask, and what did that reveal about his character?

5. What other two good leadership potentials did Peter exhibit?

6. List the five kinds of experiences the Lord brought into Peter's life after he was a disciple.

7. Give four of the six proper attitudes that Jesus taught Peter. Include a Scripture reference for each one.

8. Identify three episodes from the book of Acts that prove Peter had learned his lessons well.

Focusing on Prayer

• Pray that the young people in your church will cultivate godly potential for leadership. Pray especially for those who seem to display the most potential.

• Pray that God would grant you a humble and teachable spirit so you might learn from the difficult experiences He permits you to go through.

Applying the Truth

Meditate on 2 Peter 1:4-8. Write down each of the virtues Peter mentions. Prayerfully consider how you are doing in each area, and look for opportunities in the coming months to practice the ones you are weak in. Record what happens and what you learn.

CHAPTER 10:
PAUL: TRANSFORMED FOR FAITHFUL MINISTRY

Summarizing the Truth

Paul's remarkable spiritual conversion was unmistakably genuine from the beginning. It had far-reaching implications for the extension of the early church and the establishment in his epistles of principles that are still God's standard for ministry.

Getting Started (Choose One)

1. What hope does Paul's amazing transformation offer for today's culture? What does it clearly say about the real solution to current problems? Discuss the impact such a high-profile conversion would have on contemporary centers of power (i.e., the media, governments, schools, etc.).

2. How valuable is zeal and enthusiasm on the job, at school, in athletics, etc.? Recall a time when it was especially helpful. Not so helpful. How would you rate your current enthusiasm level?

Answering the Questions

1. Summarize Paul's personal, religious, and academic background.

2. In what context is Paul (Saul) first mentioned in the book of Acts?

3. What theological principle is always at work in conversion?

4. What sin, unless repented of, will always condemn someone to hell?

5. What made the genuineness of Paul's salvation apparent from the beginning?

6. During the first days of his new salvation, what did Paul find to be an automatic response to his new faith?

7. What fundamental truth about spiritual service did Paul understand early in his Christian life and then demonstrate throughout his ministry?

8. In what two major ways did the Holy Spirit transform Paul's life?

9. Why did Paul go away for three years to the desert shortly after his conversion?

10. Who finally convinced the other apostles to accept Paul?

11. What was the foundational attitude that Paul knew a servant of Christ needs?

12. What three realities caused Paul the most internal suffering and tears?

13. What two contemporaries of Paul could attest that he played no favorites in his teaching ministry?

14. What generally characterized Paul's evangelism? What two essential components did it always include?

15. What was the only thing in life that mattered to Paul?

Focusing on Prayer

• Thank the Lord that His sovereign grace can change even the most hardened and rebellious hearts, such as Paul's.

• Ask God to make you and everyone at your church as faithful and thorough in ministry as Paul was.

Applying the Truth

Carefully read through each of the three different accounts of Paul's conversion (Acts 9:1-30; 22:1-16; 26:4-18). Notice the similarities and differences as you compare the three. Select a fact from each passage to meditate on and apply in a way that would improve your own testimony and ministry.

CHAPTER 11:
LYDIA: THE GIFT OF FAITH

Summarizing the Chapter

Lydia's life is a succinct scriptural example of one truly set free from sin and death by the divine power of the Gospel.

Getting Started (Choose One)

1. What is your opinion of the modern women's movement? What good has it done for society? What harm?

2. Has a closed door of opportunity ever resulted in a better opportunity for you elsewhere? Describe what happened, and tell what you learned from the experience.

Answering the Questions

1. What is the only real source of personal fulfillment (see John 1:12-13; 8:32)?

2. What part of Greece did the Holy Spirit direct Paul and his companions to minister to?

3. What famous Roman highway led to Philippi?

4. What was one of the basic requirements for the formation of a synagogue? What was the alternate worship setting called (Acts 16:13)?

5. Was "Lydia" the woman's actual first name? If not, why not?

6. What product was Thyatira noted for? What was its source?

7. What does Lydia's conversion demonstrate about the extent of the Gospel message (see John 6:37)?

8. What other truth about the doctrine of salvation does Lydia's response verify?

9. Why was the practice of Christian hospitality so important in the days of the early church?

Focusing on Prayer

- Thank the Lord that He by His grace and mercy has liberated you from sin's bondage.
- Intensify your prayers for a lost friend or family member. Ask God that their heart would respond in faith like Lydia's did.

Applying the Truth

Obedience in baptism and showing hospitality is important for all believers. If you need to follow the Lord's command in either area, begin taking practical steps to do so. If neither applies to your situation now, seek another practical way you can demonstrate your faith to someone inside or outside your church.

CHAPTER 12:
TIMOTHY: A FAITHFUL SPIRITUAL SERVANT

Summarizing the Chapter

Timothy's faithfulness in modeling his life after the apostle Paul's makes him an example for all Christians to follow.

Getting Started (Choose One)

1. Discuss the importance of faithfulness in the workplace, the family, and the church. What problems does lack of faithfulness in those areas create? What are some of the pressures that drive people to be unfaithful?

2. What person has made the greatest impact in your life? What was it about his or her life that influenced you the most? What was the most important thing you learned from him or her?

Answering the Questions

1. Why is it important for all Christians to pass biblical truth on to others?

2. Explain why Paul wrote his last three inspired letters to Timothy and Titus.

3. Discuss how Timothy's mixed cultural and ethnic background was an asset for his ministry with Paul.

4. Why did Paul choose Timothy to minister with him?

5. What made Timothy qualified to act on Paul's behalf?

6. Explain the difference between Timothy's anxiety for the Philippians and the anxiety Paul forbids in Philippians 4:6.

7. What made Timothy different from Paul's other companions at Rome (see Phil. 2:19-21)?

8. How did the Philippians know Timothy was a man of integrity?

9. Why should a new convert not become a leader in the church?

10. Contrast Timothy's attitude toward Paul with that of the preachers Paul mentions in Philippians 1:15-17.

11. How did Timothy express his humility in relation to Paul?

12. List some of the sacrifices Timothy made to serve with Paul.

13. Should Christians expect a life free from trials and suffering? Explain your answer.

Focusing on Prayer

• It is essential that Christians pass on their faith to others, whether to their children, those whom they lead to Christ, or people in their church. Prayerfully consider whom God would have you disciple.

• Think of how God has proved Himself faithful to you. Thank Him for that faithfulness, and ask Him to teach you how to faithfully serve Him.

Applying the Truth

The chapter lists seven character traits that made Timothy a man of proven worth. Choose a couple of them that you need to work on, and prayerfully begin to follow Timothy's example. Ask another believer to hold you accountable to make the necessary changes in your life.

CHAPTER 13:
EPAPHRODITUS: A MODEL OF SACRIFICIAL SERVICE

Summarizing the Chapter

Epaphroditus' example of sacrificial service is the best and most instructive model for present-day Christians because he ministered at a level the majority of us are most familiar with.

Getting Started (Choose One)

1. Who was your first hero of any kind (government, sports, entertainment)? What hero (or heroine) actually had a personal impact on your life and made a positive difference (relative, friend, teacher, coach, pastor, etc.)? Explain how and why.

2. What title or descriptive phrase would you like others to remember you by? Do you think you exemplify it now? If so, why?

Answering the Questions

1. What probably hinders us most from appreciating and identifying with the sacrificial servants of the past?

2. What caused the Philippians to send Epaphroditus to Paul? What all did they ask him to do?

3. Name the three main qualities of Epaphroditus' personal character. What bearing did these have on his assignment as messenger to Paul?

4. Outline the various facets of meaning contained in the title "my brother."

5. Why was the Greek title "fellow-soldier" such an honorable one?

6. What are the two primary Greek meanings for "minister?" Why was this such a fitting title for Epaphroditus?

7. Elaborate briefly on the meaning of the expression "was distressed." How and when did that once apply to Jesus (Matt. 26:38)?

8. What exactly happened to Epaphroditus so that Paul could say he was "sick to the point of death"? What is the primary meaning of "sick," and what are some of its ramifications?

9. Why was Epaphroditus so willing to be placed in a difficult position for Paul (Phil. 2:30)?

10. What attitude was to accompany the Philippians' reception of Epaphroditus when he returned to Philippi?

Focusing on Prayer

• Pray for several missionaries you know who are serving in particularly difficult fields. Ask God that they would persevere in their sacrificial service and that they would sense His approval in some tangible way.

• Ask God to give you the dedication and humility to be worthy of some of the same titles that Paul bestowed on Epaphroditus.

Applying the Truth

From your local Christian bookstore or church library obtain and read a biography of one of the men mentioned at the outset of this chapter. (Or you can read about some other sacrificial Christian servant from the past.) Share some of your key insights with a friend; then seek to apply what you've learned to your own ministry.

CHAPTER 14:
JESUS CHRIST: THE ULTIMATE EXAMPLE OF FAITH

Summarizing the Chapter

Utilizing the metaphor of running a race (Heb. 12:1), believers are to set aside all hindrances and strive to run with excellence the race of faith. If we do that by focusing on Jesus Christ, the author and perfecter of faith, we will enjoy the fruits of spiritual victory.

Getting Started (Choose One)

1. Advertisers, especially on radio and television, use many metaphors for different aspects of life. Do you think advertising generally con-

veys these messages well? What do you most like and dislike about them? Why?

2. Do you think striving for excellence can ever degenerate into being obsessed with trying to be perfect? Would that be bad? Why or why not? In what aspect of a job or hobby do you strive to be perfect?

Answering the Questions

1. What was one of the apostle Paul's favorite metaphors for the Christian life (1 Cor. 9:24)?

2. Who makes up the "cloud of witnesses surrounding us" in Hebrews 12:1?

3. What does the Greek word for *race* include in its meaning?

4. What famous Olympic event may the Christian life be equated with?

5. As a believer, what should be your standard of performance for every aspect of life?

6. What is the key to successful Christian endurance (see Eph. 6:16)?

7. List several things that could be included as spiritual encumbrances (see Heb. 12:1). What encumbrance was the writer of Hebrews likely referring to for the Jewish believers?

8. How did the Galatian churches need to maximize their potential in order to successfully run the Christian race?

9. What specific sin most easily and frequently hinders believers as they seek to run the race?

10. What tendency from our society often diverts our attention from the ultimate goal of the Christian race?

11. Further define what is meant by the expression that Jesus is "the author . . . of faith."

12. What kind of completion is included in the truth that Jesus is the "perfecter" of faith?

13. What two realities motivated Jesus as He obediently carried out the Father's will while on earth? How and why ought these to be our motivation as well (cite several Scriptures)?

Focusing on Prayer

- Ask the Lord to help you run with renewed endurance the race of faith and to identify and throw off anything that is hindering you.
- Thank God for providing His Son to be "the author and perfecter of [our] faith" and the ultimate example we can look to as we run the race.

Applying the Truth

Drivers in long automobile races make periodic pit stops and also have others chart their progress during the race. Keep a notebook for a two-week period in which you monitor your progress each day in the race of faith. Each evening write down things that were challenges or hindrances to running with excellence. Record how you dealt with them, and note how you might improve this in the future. Read, meditate on, and memorize some of the key verses mentioned in chapter 14.

SCRIPTURE

INDEX

GENERAL

INDEX

Mary, 53, 74, 76; as mother of John the Baptist, 53, 74, 84; pregnancy of, 74-75
Elkanah, 54-56, 61; devoutness of, 55
Elliot, Jim, 139
Enoch, 19, 23
Ephaphroditus, 9, 139-46; distress of, 143-44; as Paul's *apostolos* (messenger), 142; as Paul's "brother," 141; as Philippian elder, 140-45; qualities of, 140, 144, 146; sacrificial living of, 139-40
Ephesus, 117, 129; church of, 129; elders in, 115-18
Ephraim, 54
Euphrates River, 14, 24
evangelism, 65, 69, 103, 113, 117-18, 122, 131
Ezekiel, prophetic mission of, 63

Fall, the, 17
feasts, 54-55
firstborn, deaths of, 42, 49
Flood, the, 14, 16-17, 19

Gabriel, the angel, 74, 76
Galatia, 128; churches of, 151-52; letter to the church at, 129, 152
Garden of Gethsemane, 96, 101, 143, 154
Genesis: An Expositional Commentary, 13-14, 21
Genesis, chronology of, 28-29
Gentiles, the, 29, 45, 63, 66, 71, 90, 98, 110, 116, 122, 124; Gospel opened to, 98; Paul's ministry to, 110; Peter's ministry to, 98; repentance of, 66, 70-71
God, attributes of, 18, 27, 50, 60, 66, 69, 80; authority of, 59; command of, 14, 24-25; covenant with Abraham, 28-30; covenant with Noah, 16-17; as Creator, 102; faith in, 11, 27, 32; as the Father, 23, 86, 154-55; favor with, 13; as giver of spiritual graces, 23; grace of, 18, 27, 70; judgment of, 18, 50, 63; judgment message of, 18-20, 64-65; kingdom of, 38, 43, 74, 85, 90, 92-94, 98, 121, 131, 135, 142; mercy of, 50, 69-70, 144; salvation message of 41, 72; patience of, 18; Persons of, 23, 77; presence of, 69; warning of, 149; wisdom of, 81; wrath of, 18; written law of, 35
God's Word, 7, 117, 153
Gold Cord, 136
good works, 11
Gospel, the (good news), 18, 29, 72, 98, 103, 105, 112-13, 115, 118-19, 122, 124-25, 127, 134-34, 141

Gospels, the, 92, 95-96

Hagar, 25
Hannah, 9, 53-61; background of, 54-55; and the desire for a son, 56; as faithful mother, 53-54; former barrenness of, 54-60; godly virtues of, 56-62; home relationships of, 60-62; as mother of Samuel, 61; Nazirite vow of, 58; patience of, 59-60; praise hymn of, 60, 76; prayerfulness of, 57; promise of, 57-58; purity of, 58-59; responsibility of, 60-62; as a woman of praise, 60
Haran, 24, 26
health-and-wealth gospel, 136
heaven, 23
Hebrews "Hall of Fame of the Faithful," 45, 147; writer of, 40, 147-52
hell, 23
Hellenistic Jews, 114
Holy Spirit, 11, 17, 19, 23, 26, 33, 64, 74-75, 81, 84, 86, 107, 111, 118-19, 146, 150; as inspirer of Bible authors, 123; as giver of gifts, 111, 146
hope, 31; messianic, 36
hospitality, Christian, 125; Middle Eastern, 47

idolatry, 59
The Imitation of Christ, 105
Isaac, 25-26, 30-31, 85; as the promised son, 25
Isaiah, 63, 77; prophetic mission of, 63
Ishmael, 25, 26; Arab descendants of, 25
Israel, 36-37, 63-66, 94, 123, 149; missionary call of, 63-65; as the Northern Kingdom, 64; promises for, 36-38; prophetic exhortations to, 63; religious leaders of, 88, 92, 124; shame of, 65; twelve tribes of, 96

Jacob, 26, 85
James (of the Twelve), 74, 97
James the apostle, 11
Japheth, 12
Jeremiah, prophetic mission of, 63, 136
Jericho, 45-50; destruction of, 49; pagan culture of, 47, 50
Jeroboam II, 64
Jerusalem, 55, 91, 98-99, 106, 112-14, 118-19, 129
Jesus, 9-10, 17, 23, 27-28, 30, 40-41, 53, 75, 80-81, 83, 85, 93, 95-119, 121-22, 124-25, 127, 129-37, 139, 143-56; as Abraham's descendant, 30; as the

prophetic voice of, 63; rejection of worldly pleasure and prestige, 37-41; sufferings of, 40
motherhood, high calling of, 53

Nahum, prophetic mission of, 63, 65
Nazirite vow, 58, 88-89
Nazirites, 58, 88-89
New Testament, the, 9, 23, 76, 96, 98, 105, 115, 129, 137, 140, 146-47; believers, 8-9, 146, 148; examples, 9, 139; women, 121
Newton, John, 105; conversion of, 104; in *101 Hymn Stories,* 105; writer of "Amazing Grace," 105
Nile River, 36
Nineveh, 63-71; culture of, 65; population of, 65, 70; as Syria's capital, 64; threatened punishment of, 65, 70
Ninevites, 66, 68, 70-71; repentance of, 70
Noah, 9, 11-21, 23, 36, 45, 85, 153; covenant with God, 16-17; faithful perseverance of, 14; legacy of righteousness of, 12, 20; as patriarch, 12; as "preacher of righteousness," 18; pre-Flood ministry of, 19; reverence of, 15; sons of, 12, 16; response of to God's command, 12-15

Obadiah, prophetic mission of, 63
Obed, 53; as Christ's ancestor, 53
Old Testament, the, 9, 18, 35, 49, 59, 63, 70, 76, 92, 113; chronology of, 29; examples, 40, 45; Law (see also *Mosaic Law*), 123; prophets, 63, 85, 89, 93; saints of, 8-9, 248
101 Hymn Stories, 105
Osbeck, Kenneth W., 105; writer of *101 Hymn Stories,* 105

Passover, the, 42
Paul (Saul), the apostle, 7-9, 12, 18, 27, 29-30, 105-119, 128-47, 149-53, 155; apostleship of, 110-11; background of, 105-106; conversion of, 106-109; as evangelist, 117-18; fellowship of, 112; as filled with the Spirit, 111-12; first missionary journey, 124; humility of, 11, 134; imprisonment, 129, 140-41, 145; instruction by, 117; letters written by, 107-108, 110-13, 115-18, 129-33; Macedonian vision of, 122; as a Pharisee, 106; as persecutor, 106-107; as the persecuted, 113-14, 117; prayer of, 109; preaching of, 112-113, 124; as role

model, 131; Roman citizenship of, 105; sacrificial attitude of, 118-19; second missionary journey of, 122; servanthood of, 115; service of, 110-11, 115-19; suffering of, 116-17
Peninnah, 54-56; as Hannah's rival, 55
Penn, William, 87
Peter, the apostle, 8-9, 18, 95-104, 117; background of, 97; character of, 97; as courageous spokesman, 103; denial of Christ, 97, 99-100; divine revelations given to, 98; faith of, 95, 103; as future judge of Israel, 96; learned attitudes of, 100-104; names of, 96; as object of rebukes, 98-99; perseverance of, 103; *protos* (first in rank) status of, 95-96, 102; questions of, 97; recommissioning of, 99-102; strengths and weaknesses of, 95-104
Pharaoh, 25, 39, 148; daughter of, 36-37
Pharisees, 87-88
Philippi, 122-23, 140, 142-44; church at, 123, 129-34, 136, 140-45, 149; Jewish community of, 122-23
Philippians, the Letter to, 9, 129-30, 132-36, 141, 149, 194
Philistines, the, 53
plagues, on Pharaoh due to Abraham, 25; the ten, 42
Pollock, John, 38; *More Than Conquerors,* 39
polygamy, 54
polytheism, 24
pre-Flood believers, 23; days, 20; descendants (Adam through Seth), 12-13, 20
Prodigal Son, the, 69
Promised Land, the, 26, 36, 38, 41, 46
prophets, major and minor, 63; Old Testament, 63, 85, 89, 93
proselytes, Gentile, 92
A Puritan Golden Treasury, 136

"Queen of Heaven," the, 73, 79

race of faith, the, 149-56; agony of, 149; encumbrances to, 151-52; endurance needed to run, 149-50; rewards of, 154-56; goal of, 152-56
Rachel, 53
Rahab, 9, 45-51; escape from divine wrath of, 50; faith of, 48-51; as Gentile prostitute, 45; as great-grandmother of David, 45; and the Hebrew spies, 47-51; lie of, 47; scarlet cord of, 49; vindication of, 49-51
Ramah, 61